CONTENTS

IRISH VOLUNTEER SOLDIER 1913–23

INTRODUCTION

Martin Walton joined the Irish Volunteers just three weeks before the Easter Rebellion in 1916. Though a mere 15 years of age, his height enabled him to fool the attesting officer and he enlisted as an adult. Thereafter, he had attended only two meetings and received minimal instruction on how to handle a rifle before Captain Con Colbert called at his house on Easter Monday morning with orders to report to his unit. Walton never received the message because he had gone to get a tooth removed but when news of the Rebellion began to filter through that night he decided he was duty-bound to travel into the city centre the following morning, despite his parents' removal of the valves from his bicycle tyres in an attempt to deter him.

Eventually arriving in O'Connell Street he found, not violent rebellion, but looters emptying several shops of their contents and the air reeking with the rancid smell of dead horses rotting where they had fallen, shot from under the Lancers as they had charged at the General Post Office (GPO) the day before. When Walton eventually found his unit, C Company of the 2nd Battalion, they were holed up in Jacob's Biscuit Factory on Wexford Street, surrounded not by the British Army but by an irate mob screaming abuse at them and demanding that they come out, go to France, and fight in a real war. However, within hours this under-age Volunteer would also find himself embroiled in a real war when General Lowe embarked on operations to restore British authority in the capital.

Very few photographs were taken of the Irish Volunteers during the Easter Rebellion. This photograph is one which actually survived from the GPO. (Irish Military Archives)

The first military operation undertaken by the Volunteers was the landing of 900 Mauser rifles and 26,000 rounds of ammunition at Howth Pier in County Dublin on 26 July 1914. Although discovered by the security forces, the Volunteers still managed to carry the weapons to storage points by strapping them to the crossbars of their bicycles. These weapons were to form the main armament of the Volunteer Movement. (National Museum of Ireland)

Fortunately for Walton, Lowe's main thrust would focus on the GPO, where machine-guns, incendiary shells, 18-pounder artillery pieces, and the gunboat *Helga* were all employed in a concentration of fire designed to batter those inside into capitulation. It worked, and many Volunteers died in the process. Deployed within the biscuit factory, Martin Walton was spared this savagery. He was destined to survive the Rebellion and its aftermath having played his own unique part in the Irish Volunteer Movement.

CHRONOLOGY

8 April 1886	William Gladstone introduces First Home Rule Bill for Ireland in the House of Commons – it fails to gain necessary majority.
13 February 1893	Second Home Rule Bill introduced by Gladstone – vetoed by the House of Lords.
5 May 1905	Arthur Griffith founds the Sinn Fein political party in Dublin.
11 April 1912	Third Home Rule Bill introduced by Lloyd George.
13 January 1913	Ulster Volunteer Force formed in Belfast.
25 November 1913	Inaugural meeting of the Irish Volunteers held in Dublin.
26 July 1914	Irish Volunteers land a shipment of 900 rifles and 26,000 rounds of ammunition at Howth, County Dublin.
1 August 1914	Outbreak of First World War.
18 September 1914	Third Home Rule Bill placed on the Statute Book – implementation suspended until the end of the war.
20 September 1914	John Redmond, leader of the Irish Parliamentary Party, urges the Irish Volunteers to enlist in the British Army. This leads to a split in the Volunteer Movement. The majority (170,000) follow Redmond and are renamed the 'National Volunteers'. The minority (12,000) retain the title of 'Irish Volunteers'.
24–29 April 1916	The Easter Rebellion.
11 November 1918	Armistice comes into effect, ending the First World War.
14 December 1918	General election in Britain and Ireland. The Sinn Fein party wins majority of seats in Ireland and vows to set up a separate assembly called *Dail Eireann*.
21 January 1919	*Dail Eireann* meets for the first time in the Mansion House in Dublin as the Anglo-Irish War commences with an attack on Royal Irish Constabulary (RIC) barracks at Soloheadbeg, County Tipperary.

20 August 1919	The Irish Volunteers are brought under governmental control and are required to swear allegiance to *Dail Eireann* and the Irish Republic. This practice did not become widespread until June 1920.
2 January 1920	Recruitment commences in Britain for retired servicemen to serve in Ireland as police reinforcements.
25 February 1920	Government of Ireland Bill introduced in the House of Commons. This Bill provided for separate parliaments in the North and South.
25 March 1920	On arrival in Ireland new police reinforcements are dressed in a mixture of dark green Royal Irish Constabulary (RIC) uniforms and British Army khaki – earning them the nickname 'Black and Tans'.
27 July 1920	Recruitment commences in Britain for an auxiliary division of the RIC to be comprised of ex-British officers with combat experience.
20 October 1920	The House of Commons is informed that between 1 January 1919 and 18 October 1920 the Volunteers had destroyed 64 courthouses and forced the evacuation of 492 RIC barracks. Crown casualties to that point had totalled 23 soldiers dead and 71 wounded, with 117 members of the RIC killed and 185 wounded.
25 October 1920	The Lord Mayor of Cork, Terence MacSwiney, dies in Brixton Prison on the 74th day of a hunger strike.
21 November 1920	Members of Michael Collins' 'Squad' shoot dead 14 British intelligence agents in Dublin. In response the Auxiliaries retaliate by shooting dead three Volunteers, and a party of 'Black and Tans' enter Croke Park Stadium during a Gaelic football match and open fire on the crowd, killing 12 people. This day became known in republican folklore as 'Bloody Sunday'.
28 November 1920	The 3rd Cork Brigade Flying Column attacks a convoy of 18 Auxiliaries at Kilmichael, County Cork, killing 17 of them.
10 December 1920	Martial Law is declared in counties Cork, Kerry, Limerick and Tipperary.
28 February 1921	Six Volunteer prisoners are executed in Victoria Barracks, Cork. The Volunteers shoot six British soldiers in Cork City in retaliation.
19 March 1921	The 3rd Cork Brigade Flying Column successfully ambush Crown forces at Crossbarry, County Cork, causing many casualties.
11 July 1921	The Truce comes into effect, bringing an end to the Anglo-Irish War.
14 September 1921	*Dail Eireann* selects five delegates to negotiate and conclude a settlement with the British Government.
6 December 1921	A Treaty between Great Britain and Ireland is concluded and signed. Southern Ireland to be granted 'dominion' status. It will be known as the Irish Free State and will have its own parliament, judiciary and defence force. An oath of allegiance to the king will be required by all elected representatives. The six counties of Northern Ireland are to be a separate state with its own parliament.
7 January 1922	*Dail Eireann* approves the Anglo-Irish Treaty by 64 votes to 57.
10 January 1922	Eamon de Valera is defeated in vote for presidency of the *Dail* by 60 votes to 58 and leads his followers from the chamber.
14 January 1922	Pro-Treaty *Dail* deputies meet and approve resolutions establishing a provisional government which is recognised by Great Britain. Michael Collins is appointed chairman; Richard Mulcahy is Minister for Defence, and General Eoin O'Duffy becomes Chief-of-Staff of the new National Army.
16 January 1922	The Lord-Lieutenant formally hands over power to Michael Collins at a ceremony in Dublin Castle. The Volunteers now begin to divide along pro- and anti-Treaty lines.
31 January 1922	The National Army takes over Beggar's Bush Barracks, Dublin, from the British Army and establishes its headquarters there.

9 April 1922	Anti-Treaty delegates attend an 'army convention' in Dublin electing their own 'army executive' with Liam Lynch becoming the alternative Chief-of-Staff.
13 April 1922	Anti-Treaty forces occupy the Four Courts in Dublin.
1 May 1922	Senior National Army officers meet with anti-Treaty officers and sign a document aimed at unification of the army.
16 June 1922	General election held in the Irish Free State. A majority of those elected are in favour of the Anglo-Irish Treaty.
22 June 1922	Sir Henry Wilson, military advisor to the government of Northern Ireland, is assassinated in London. The British Government calls on the Provisional Irish Government to take action against dissident forces.
28 June 1922	Free State forces commence an artillery bombardment of the anti-Treaty forces occupying the Four Courts in Dublin. This action marks the beginning of the Irish Civil War.
1–5 July 1922	Heavy fighting in Dublin as the National Army fights to gain control of the city.
5 July 1922	Government issues a national call to arms.
12 July 1922	Government forms a war council – Michael Collins is appointed Commander-in-Chief of the National Army.
20 July 1922	National Army captures Limerick and Waterford cities.
2 August 1922	In the first of a series of seaborne landings behind a defensive screen established by the anti-Treaty forces, 450 members of the Dublin Guards unit of the National Army land at Fenit, County Kerry.
8 August 1922	Further landings by units of the National Army occur at Passage West, Youghal, and Union Hall in County Cork.
11 August 1922	Cork City captured by National Army.
22 August 1922	Michael Collins is shot dead during an ambush at *Beal na mBlath* in West Cork.
18 January 1923	Liam Deasy, a prominent leader of the anti-Treaty forces, is captured by the National Army and issues a document calling for an immediate and unconditional surrender.
10 April 1923	Liam Lynch, Chief-of-Staff of the anti-Treaty forces, is shot and mortally wounded by units of the National Army in the Knockmealdown mountains. Lynch is succeeded by Frank Aiken.
30 April 1923	Aiken orders all anti-Treaty forces to suspend offensive operations.
24 May 1923	Aiken orders a ceasefire and instructs all anti-Treaty units to dump their arms. This marks the end of the Civil War.
3 August 1923	The Defence Forces (Temporary Provisions) Act 1923 comes into force placing the army on a statutory footing.
22 August 1923	A huge National Army victory parade is held in Phoenix Park, Dublin.

Founded in January 1913 to resist the introduction of Home Rule, the Ulster Volunteer Force was led by retired British officers. Membership eventually rose to 90,000 and the force was armed with weapons provided by wealthy supporters and 24,000 rifles brought ashore at the ports of Larne and Bangor on 25 April 1914. (National Museum of Ireland)

HISTORICAL BACKGROUND

Home Rule for Ireland had been the key issue that dominated political debate in both Ireland and the United Kingdom since William Gladstone introduced the First Home Rule Bill in 1886. Seven years later the Second Home Rule Bill was actually passed in the House of Commons but vetoed by the House of Lords. However, it was the Third Home Rule Bill, introduced in April 1912, which sparked off a crisis in Ireland where the majority Nationalist population had high expectations of autonomy, and the Unionists in Ulster were bitterly opposed to any such notion.

On 28 September 1912, almost 250,000 Unionists gathered at Belfast's City Hall and signed a 'Solemn League and Covenant' pledging themselves to resist the granting of Home Rule, and so intense was their opposition that some even signed the document in their own blood. This was quickly followed in January 1913 by the formation of the Ulster Volunteer Force, an organisation composed of adult male Unionists who were prepared to resist Home Rule by force of arms if necessary.

Not surprisingly this development immediately alarmed Nationalist Ireland where, in contrast to the Unionists, and in order to safeguard the granting of Home Rule, the Irish Volunteers (*Oglaigh na hEireann* in Irish) were formed at a huge public meeting held at the Rotunda Rink in Dublin on 25 November 1913. The concept of such a body had been previously mooted in an article published in the Gaelic League journal, *An Claidheamh Soluis* (The Sword of Light), by Eoin MacNeill, professor of Early and Medieval Irish History at University College Dublin, who became the Volunteer Movement's first elected chief-of-staff.

One of the many notices posted all over Dublin announcing the formation of the Irish Volunteers. This meeting attracted huge crowds and was addressed by the prominent nationalists Eoin MacNeill, Patrick Pearse, and Michael Davitt. (National Museum of Ireland)

However, right from the beginning, this new movement also included members of the shadowy Irish Republican Brotherhood (IRB), a secret oath-bound society dedicated to establishing an independent Irish Republic by force of arms. The IRB leadership viewed the Volunteers as the ideal means by which to achieve their aims and, before long, several of their number had found their way into prominent positions within the Volunteer leadership. In the years that followed, the role of the IRB within the movement would prove critical.

Within six months of its inaugural meeting the strength of the Volunteers had risen to 75,000 with units formed in most parts of the country. John Redmond, leader of the majority Irish Parliamentary Party, was slow to give the movement his support. However, in June 1914, and in the interests of harmony, the Volunteer leadership reluctantly agreed to permit him to nominate half the membership of its executive. This move immediately brought in further Volunteer recruits and the strength quickly rose to over 160,000.

But it was the outbreak of the First World War that was to have far-reaching consequences both for the Volunteer Movement and for Ireland as a whole. In

September 1914 the Third Home Rule Bill was signed by King George V and placed on the Statute Book to be implemented 12 months later, or at the end of the war, whichever was the later date. In response, Redmond made an impassioned plea at the village of Woodenbridge, County Wicklow, on 20 September 1914 in which he advocated that members of the Volunteer Movement enlist in the British Army.

The response was overwhelming but it split the organisation; 170,000 answered Redmond's call and were promptly renamed the 'National Volunteers' and thousands of their number went to serve with great distinction in the 10th and 16th Divisions of the British Army. The more militant minority, of which there were initially 12,000, refused to follow suit. This group, who for the most part were dominated by the IRB, retained the title of 'Irish Volunteers' and, subscribing to the ideology that 'England's difficulty was Ireland's opportunity', established its own military council in 1915. Under the leadership of Patrick Pearse, they now set about planning rebellion against the Crown in order to establish an independent Irish Republic.

ENLISTMENT

When the inaugural meeting of the Irish Volunteers was held in November 1913, so great was interest in the new force that a crowd of over 7,000 tried to gain admission. The Rotunda Rink held 4,000 and was filled to capacity, leaving over 3,000 more outside, where a separate meeting was held in the nearby public gardens. When the speeches finished, stewards mingled with both crowds, distributing enrolment forms and in excess of 3,000 adult males immediately enlisted. Thereafter, a series of meetings held throughout the country also attracted huge numbers, and by the end of August 1914 the movement could claim an active strength of just over 180,000. For these Volunteers the objective of the movement as set out in its 1913 manifesto was unambiguous. They were joining to 'secure and maintain the rights and

Patrick Pearse, the Volunteers' Director of Organisation and leader of the IRB Military Council, addresses a meeting in 1915 advocating his own brand of Irish nationalism. (Irish Military Archives)

liberties common to all the people of Ireland' at a time when political and social uncertainty were the order of the day. This ideology attracted recruits from all shades of nationalist opinion, with members of existing organisations such as the Gaelic Athletic Association (GAA), the Gaelic League, and the Fianna Eireann youth movement all viewing the Volunteers as the vehicle to promote their own cultural causes. Equally, supporters of Redmond and the Irish Parliamentary Party also saw the Volunteers as the perfect mechanism to secure Home Rule.

However, after the split with Redmond the minority 'Irish Volunteer' grouping was faced with the daunting task of rebuilding the organisation and commenced a nationwide campaign to attract new recruits. Unlike their counterparts in the British Army they did not have any established recruiting offices and were forced instead to rely on alternative methods. Periodicals such as *The Irish Volunteer* were used to publicise the aims of the organisation, and public parades, such as those held throughout the country on Saint Patrick's Day, proved very successful in attracting recruits when local Volunteer units took to the streets accompanied by pipe bands.

Those wishing to enlist then had to sign the following enrolment form:

I, the undersigned, desire to be enrolled for service in Ireland as a member of the Irish Volunteer Force. I subscribe to the Constitution of the Irish Volunteers and pledge my willing obedience to every article of it. I declare that in joining the Irish Volunteer Force I set before myself the stated objects of the Irish Volunteers and no others.

The order issued to the Cork Brigade by Commandant Tomas MacCurtain for the 1916 Saint Patrick's Day demonstration emphasising the importance of discipline. Such occasions were used to promote the aims of the Volunteer Movement and to attract new recruits. (Dara McGrath/Cork Public Museum)

1. To secure and maintain the rights and liberties common to all the peoples of Ireland.

2. To train, discipline, and equip for this purpose an Irish Volunteer Force which will render service to an Irish National Government when such is established.

3. To unite in the service of Ireland Irishmen of every creed and of every party and class.

Once attested, individual members were then issued with a membership card and copies of *The Irish Volunteer Handbook* and *The General Scheme of Organisation*. They were also required to pay a weekly subscription, which was recorded on their membership card, and this money, together with subscriptions received from abroad, enabled units to rent offices and halls for administrative and training purposes.

Printed by P. Mayes, 3 Marshall Street, Dublin

741 Óglaiġ na hÉireann—Irish Volunteers
"B" COY., 5th BATTN. GALWAY REGIMENT.

DRAWING OF PRIZES (In Aid of Equipment Fund)

At HEADQUARTERS, BALLYNAHALAN, GORT, Co. GALWAY,

On FRIDAY, 17th MARCH, 1916, at 7 o'clock p.m.

1st Prize—A MAGAZINE RIFLE

SECOND PRIZE—
A HARRINGTON & R. REVOLVER
.22 Cal., nickelled 3-inch barrel.

THIRD PRIZE—
A BEAUTIFUL PIKE HEAD,
of the best Kt-steel, nicely finished.

Ticket - Sixpence Each.

Winning numbers will be published in the "Irish Volunteer" of March 25th, 1916.

Raffles held by different units often had the dual purpose of raising funds and providing arms and equipment to the membership. (Author's collection)

The overwhelming majority of those who enlisted were Roman Catholic, aged between 20 and 30, and from a working- or middle-class background. Officers, on the other hand, tended to be slightly older, better educated and more financially secure. Later, as the Anglo-Irish War progressed, the average age of those enlisting dropped slightly and the difference in background largely disappeared.

While recruitment became less visible after the Easter Rebellion, the surge in public support for the movement saw increased numbers wishing to join, and the British Government's threat to extend conscription to Ireland in 1918 had similar predictable effects. However, once the war had concluded, many of these latter-day Volunteer enthusiasts soon drifted away from the movement. Nevertheless, recruiting continued throughout the Anglo-Irish War, the only significant change being that from June 1920 onwards new recruits were required to swear an oath of allegiance to *Dail Eireann* and the Irish Republic. The signing of the Truce in July 1921 brought in more Volunteers, some of whom had been too young to take part in the war, while others now joining for the first time could certainly have taken part in the fighting had they wished to do so. Veterans of the war contemptuously dismissed the latter as 'Trucileers'.

Recruitment for the new National Army commenced in January 1922 and recruiting officers were able to utilise the machinery of state, together with the resources of the media, to attract young men into the organisation. On 5 July 1922, the Provisional Government issued a nationwide call to arms in an effort to attract new recruits and the response was dramatic as hundreds of young men began presenting themselves at the different recruiting centres each day.

There were many reasons why so many chose a military career at this particular time. Some did so out of a sense of patriotism or a yearning

A contingent of Dublin Volunteers parade carrying some of the rifles landed at Howth Pier. Prior to the introduction of uniforms Volunteers paraded wearing civilian clothing with bandoliers and haversacks. (National Museum of Ireland)

for adventure. More saw a career in the army as helping to alleviate the deprivations being endured as a result of unemployment, while others joined simply because they had previously served in the British Army and wished to continue in military life. In this regard, General Emmet Dalton noted in his report of 11 September 1922 to the commander-in-chief that, following the sea landings and capture of Cork, he had recruited a total of 350 such ex-servicemen. Whatever the case, the army provided all of them with food, accommodation and a steady wage, and offered a stability in their lives that was not available elsewhere at the time. By the end of the Civil War the strength of the National Army had risen to 60,000 all ranks.

ORGANISATION

The first Volunteer units were called 'corps', 'brigades' or 'regiments'. However, as the organisation expanded, and then split, it quickly became necessary to put in place a more precise form of military structure. When the first Convention of the Irish Volunteers assembled in the Abbey Theatre, Dublin, on Sunday 25 October 1914 it was agreed that the movement would be governed by a general council of 50 members who would meet monthly, and a nine-man central executive which would meet on a weekly basis. At the Executive's inaugural meeting on 25 November 1914 a committee of military organisation was appointed and tasked with drafting a proposal for the establishment of a general headquarters (GHQ).

These proposals, approved by the Central Executive on 5 December 1914 and later endorsed by the General Council, allowed for the establishment of a GHQ staff comprising a chief-of-staff, a quartermaster-general and directors of organisation, military operations, training, and arms. Two further appointments were sanctioned the following year, a chief-of-inspection and director of communications. GHQ would hold responsibility for the overall operation of the Irish Volunteers until the establishment of the National Army in 1922.

It was also in December 1914 that a 'Scheme of Military Organisation' was adopted by the General Council which saw the main Volunteer tactical unit designated as a 'company'. This was then divided into two 'half-companies', each with two 'sections', which in turn contained two eight-man squads and a number of specialists. The total company establishment was 103, all ranks.

Company officers:	
Company Commander	1 Captain
Half-company Commanders	2 Lieutenants
Company Adjutant	1 Lieutenant

Subordinate officers and men:	
Section commanders	4
4 Sections x 16	64
Scout Commanders	1
Section of Cycle Scouts	16
Transport and supply	4
Ambulances	8
Company Signallers	1
Buglers/Pipers/Drummers	1

The document also made provision for the formation of Volunteer 'battalions' led by a commandant and comprising four or more companies but not exceeding eight in total. It further provided for the establishment of engineer, transport, supply and communications battalions together with a hospital corps. Volunteer brigades would be commanded by a brigadier-general and would consist of three or more battalions but not exceeding five in total.

Companies were usually drawn from small country towns or city parishes and known as 'company districts'. Companies in neighbouring districts were then grouped into battalions which were usually centred on a large town or city known as 'Battalion Districts'. Initially brigades were organised on a county basis, for example, the Cork Brigade or Limerick Brigade. Later, in 1919, the strength of some county brigades had grown so large that it was difficult for them to be controlled and administered from one headquarters, and GHQ directed that these units be divided along new territorial boundaries. For example, the Cork Brigade was divided into three new brigade formations centred in the north, west and centre of the county.

Then, at the height of the Anglo-Irish War, GHQ found it necessary to order the creation of full-time Active Service Units drawn from the existing brigade structure. Those operating in rural Ireland became known as 'Flying Columns' and formed the spearhead of the Volunteers'

Michael Collins was probably the most charismatic leader of the Volunteer Movement and was Director of both Organisation and Intelligence. Later, as part of the delegation which negotiated the Treaty, he played a crucial role and was subsequently elected Chairman of the Provisional Government. Thereafter, he was the first Commander-in-Chief of the National Army. (Irish Military Archives)

These five members of 'The Squad' took their orders from Michael Collins, eliminated numerous British agents working in Dublin, and participated in operations such as the burning of the Customs House, Dublin, in May 1921. Left to right: Michael McDonnell, Tom Keogh, Vincent Byrne, Patrick Daly and James Slattery. (Author's collection)

guerrilla offensive. However, such was the nature of the conflict that Michael Collins eventually found it necessary to establish a small team of specially selected men from his intelligence department who were primarily tasked with the execution of British agents. This group became known as 'The Squad', or 'The Twelve Apostles'.

The next formal amendment to the Volunteer organisation occurred in April 1921 when GHQ sanctioned the formation of 'divisions' with each containing a number of brigades. In a memorandum circulated at the time it was stated that the main purpose of this move was to reduce the number of units communicating with GHQ thus reducing the volume of administration and thereby enabling the GHQ staff to focus on organising greater logistical and operational co-operation between these formations. The divisional organisation remained intact until the Truce in July 1921 when the strength of the Volunteers stood at approximately 100,000.

The first unit of the new National Army was formed in January 1922 and was drawn from the Active Service Units of the Dublin Brigade and members of 'The Squad'; it was known as 'The Dublin Guards'. This unit, fully equipped and uniformed, took over Beggar's Bush Barracks from the British Army on 31 January 1922.

As the National Army evolved it adopted an operational structure based on divisions, brigades and battalions. General Order No. 1 of 5 July 1922 also created eight territorial administrative formations known as 'District Commands' and a subsequent reorganisation on 18 January 1923 divided the force into nine 'Commands'. General Order No. 16 of 24 January 1923 then provided for the creation of 65 numbered infantry battalions. Thereafter an air corps, an army medical service, an artillery corps, a corps of engineers, a railway protection, repair and maintenance corps, an independent signal corps, a military police corps, a transport corps, a supply corps, an ordnance corps, a pay corps, and an army school of music were all established.

A unit of Dublin Guards march through Phoenix Park, Dublin, *en route* to take over Beggar's Bush Barracks from the British, 30 January 1922. This was the first public appearance by the new National Army. (National Museum of Ireland/Cashman Collection)

APPEARANCE

The most notable characteristic of the Irish Volunteer soldier's appearance between 1913 and 1923 was diversity. Originally conceived as a 'national army', every effort was made to ensure uniformity of dress and early in 1914 a uniform sub-committee was appointed to draft a design for the Volunteer uniform. The first part of this task was to find material of make and colour suitable for fieldwork in Ireland. Having searched the country without success, a sample of a 'grey-green' material was found in England which was deemed to be suitable. However, most woollen mills were reluctant to take the Volunteer order as all resources at the time were being ploughed into the British war effort on the continent. Eventually the Morrogh Brothers at Douglas Woollen Mills in Cork agreed to manufacture the material, and they received the first order.

The sub-committee next turned their attention to the matter of uniform design and it was agreed that all ranks and units would wear a standard tunic with rolled collar, dark green shoulder straps and pointed cuffs, two breast patch pockets (each with a box pleat) and two patch pockets at the hips, with each shoulder reinforced with an extra patch of serge. Five large brass buttons bearing an Irish harp and the letters 'IV' would appear on the front with smaller versions on the breast pocket flaps and tunic straps. Breeches and puttees of light serge to match the tunic would also be worn and the only variation permitted would be the facings on the tunics which were left to the discretion of each regimental committee or county board. A brown leather bandolier and white canvas haversack were approved for carrying ammunition and equipment.

Head-dress would consist of a round-crowned cap with a black patent-leather peak and chin strap. A soft hat of similar pattern to that worn by the Boers in South Africa was selected for 'fieldwork' and this became known as the 'Cronje hat' after the Boer General, Piet Cronje. A brown leather belt would also be worn at the waist and fastened with

This 'approved' Volunteer tunic was worn primarily by members of the Dublin Brigade who were in a position to purchase their uniforms from a number of recognised tailors located within the city. Rural units did not have access to the same facilities. (National Museum of Ireland)

This pattern of brown leather ammunition bandolier was worn by Volunteers from the time of formation, throughout the Easter Rebellion, and during the Anglo-Irish War. (Author's collection)

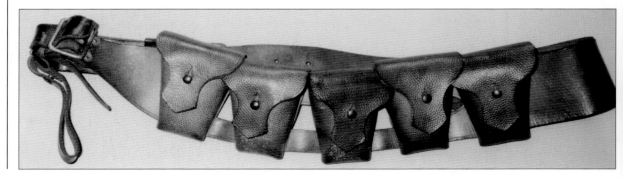

a round brass clasp with the words '*Oglaigh na hEireann*' around the edge and a harp as the centre-piece.

The first Irish Volunteer cap badge appeared early in 1914 and depicted an Irish harp. However, after the split with Redmond, several other cap badges were produced for the different brigades, each with its own distinctive pattern. Eoin MacNeill designed a cap badge for the Dublin Brigade which was worn in white metal by officers and bronze by other ranks. A variant of this badge was subsequently adopted by the entire Volunteer Movement.

When the Mooragh Brothers eventually supplied the new material, the first contract for supply of 300 Volunteer uniforms was awarded to the Limerick Clothing Factory which was in fact located at Lower Bridge Street, Dublin. It was assumed that all Volunteers wishing to purchase their uniforms would do so from this single 'approved' supplier, but a report from the 'uniform sub-committee' dated 12 August 1914 stated that, 'numbers of Volunteers have obtained uniforms elsewhere than from the official supplier and in many cases these uniforms are not of standard material or standard design'. The report went on to point out that, 'as the Volunteers were a democratic force, all uniforms should be exactly similar and that no distinction should be made between officers and other ranks as all officer appointments were temporary in nature.'

17

Nevertheless some officers of the Dublin Brigade were particularly well uniformed at an early stage with firms like Thomas Fallon & Co., of 8 Mary Street, Dublin, selling badges, head-dresses, and uniforms to individual Volunteers. Haversacks cost between tenpence and one shilling and sixpence; greatcoats were 25 shillings; Cronje hats retailed at one shilling and eightpence; and infantry swords in brown leather scabbards cost five guineas. The rank and file, however, didn't have much money to spend on their uniforms nor the luxury of a quartermaster's stores from which to draw their kit. This ensured that, despite all attempts at uniformity, the cut and colour of the uniforms that appeared tended to vary greatly. Local tailors often had to work without a pattern and use cloth that didn't match the approved colour. And the same applied to buttons, belts and buckles many of which were also made locally. Initially the rank insignia adopted were the same as those used by the British Army. Markings were on the tunic cuff with Volunteer buttons used instead of pips. These were soon replaced with shamrock clusters, referred to in regulations as 'trefoils', and a brass 'wheeled cross' with blue enamel inlay based on an emblem design dating back to a historical event known as the Confederation of Kilkenny, which took place in 1642. After 1915 all metal rank markings were replaced by embroidered versions which came in dark green, blue and yellow issues.

A major attempt to standardise the uniform was made at a meeting of the Volunteer Central Executive held in Dublin on 13 October 1915 when a new dress instruction was approved. Individual Volunteers read of this development ten days later when details were published in the *Irish Volunteer* periodical:

1. Uniform is not compulsory for Irish Volunteers, but it is desirable, especially in the case of officers.

2. Uniform will consist of tunic, breeches, puttees, and cap, of the approved design, in the approved green heather tweed, with dark green shoulder straps and cuffs. (Leggings may be substituted for puttees at option.)

An original receipt from Thomas Fallon & Co., Dublin, issued to Volunteer Charles Saurin for the purchase of a bandolier, haversack and belt. (Author's collection)

This tunic, tailor-made for Diarmuid Lynch, a Staff-Captain in the GPO, illustrates the 'open-neck' pattern worn by some officers, which was contrary to dress regulations. (Dara McGrath/Cork Public Museum)

3. All buttons will be dark green compressed leather. (Volunteers who have already brass buttons may have such buttons oxidised dark green in lieu of getting regulation buttons.) Shiny buttons, marks of rank, cap-peaks, or other shiny objects, are not to be worn.

The following system of rank markings also came into force:

Rank	Insignia	Position
Squad Commander	One dark green stripe	Left breast of tunic
Section Commander	Two dark green stripes	Left breast of tunic
Company Adjutant	Three dark green stripes	Left breast of tunic
2nd Lieutenant	One trefoil and one dark green band	Cuffs
1st Lieutenant	Two trefoils and one dark green band	Cuffs
Captain	Three trefoils and two dark green bands	Cuffs
Vice-Commandant	One wheeled cross and three dark green bands	Cuffs
Commandant	Two wheeled crosses and three dark green bands	Cuffs
Vice-Commandant-General	Two wheeled crosses and four dark green bands	Cuffs
Commandant General	Three wheeled crosses and four dark green bands	Cuffs

The failure of the Easter Rebellion and the move towards the tactics of guerrilla warfare led to a major change in the appearance of the Volunteer soldier and, with some notable exceptions such as military funerals, the wearing of the uniform in public became infrequent. Accordingly, when the Anglo-Irish War erupted in 1919, Volunteers were dressed almost entirely in civvies carrying an assortment of ancillary military equipment. Of course, there was also a functional pattern to what they wore. The majority favoured trench coats, soft hats and leggings (gaiters) as the most suitable garments for guerrilla warfare in the countryside, and for survival in Ireland's notoriously inclement weather. In most cases the officers could only be identified by the Sam Browne belts they wore over their civvies and the fact that generally they also sported a collar and tie.

However, when the Truce came into effect in July 1921 some old Volunteer uniforms reappeared as it was safe once again to wear them in public, but when recruitment began for the National Army in 1922, an entirely new uniform was authorised. For officers this consisted of a

Awaiting the issue of new uniforms, this group of National Army officers, pictured in the summer of 1922, still wear their old Volunteer uniforms. Second from the right is General Michael Brennan who once summed up his military philosophy: 'When you go to war, hit first, hit hard and hit anywhere.' (Irish Military Archives)

soft-crowned peaked cap made of dark green serge. The tunic was made from the same material, cut long in the skirt, and worn with a Sam Browne belt. It had a stand collar; two breast patch pockets with centre box pleats; two large side pockets at the hips, and shoulder straps. The breeches and trousers were again of the same material.

This time ordinary Volunteers were able to draw their kit from a quartermaster's stores and wore a uniform similar in pattern to their officers, with 'battle order' consisting of British 1908 pattern web equipment. All ranks wore brown boots and leggings with rank markings of cloth bands worn on the cuff. They were also issued for the first time with a greatcoat for bad weather and a schedule of items necessary to maintain their kit. But by far the most significant aspect of this new uniform was retention of the Irish Volunteer cap badge and tunic buttons in recognition of the new army's origins in the Volunteer Movement. But from the perspective of the ordinary Volunteer it was the functionality of the uniform that mattered most. He now possessed clothing and accoutrements which were suitable for everyday dress, ceremonial occasions, and service in the field.

The new rank insignia in 1922 was made of cloth and worn in the form of cuff bands for all ranks up to general officer. Cap badges were worn on a diamond-shaped cloth backing, coloured in accordance with rank.

Rank	Cuff bands	Cloth cap diamonds
Volunteer	None	None
Corporal	One green	Green
Sergeant	Two green	Green
Sergeant-Major	Three green	Green
2nd Lieutenant	One blue	Blue
Lieutenant	Two blue	Blue
Captain	Three blue	Blue
Vice-Commandant (battalion)	Two purple	Purple
Lieutenant-Commandant (brigade)	Two brown	Brown
Lieutenant-Commandant (division)	Two red	Red
Commandant (battalion)	Three purple	Purple
Commandant (brigade)	Three brown	Brown
Commandant (division)	Three red	Red
Brigadier	Two brown with narrow gold band between	Brown
Colonel-Commandant	Two red bands with narrow gold band between	Red

Rank insignia for General Officers consisted of cloth bands worn on the shoulder strap together with collar gorget and cloth cap diamonds.

Rank	Shoulder bands	Collar gorget	Cap diamonds
Division Commandant-General	One gold band between two red bands	Red and gold	Yellow
GHQ Commandant-General	One gold band	Yellow	Yellow
GHQ Major-General	Two gold bands (one wide, one narrow)	Gold and yellow	Yellow
GHQ Lieutenant-General	Two gold bands	Gold and yellow	Yellow
GHQ General	Three gold bands	Gold and yellow	Yellow

In January 1923 a further reorganisation of the National Army's rank structure took place. General Routine Order No. 19 of 31 January 1923 laid down the following 'Re-arrangement of Rank and Insignia':

Rank	Insignia	Position
Private	Nil	
Corporal	One green bar	Sleeve of left arm
Sergeant	Two green bars	Sleeve of left arm
Sergeant-Major	Three green bars	Sleeve of left arm
2nd Lieutenant	One blue bar	Shoulder strap
Lieutenant	Two blue bars	Shoulder strap
Captain	Three blue bars	Shoulder strap
Commandant	Two red bars	Shoulder strap
Colonel	Three red bars	Shoulder strap and collar
Major-General	Two red bars with one gold bar between	Shoulder strap and collar
Lieutenant-General	Two gold bars	Shoulder strap and collar
General	Three gold bars	Shoulder strap and collar

Additionally it was required that all officers be recommissioned and they were not permitted to wear the new insignia until their names had been published in General Routine Order No. 23 of 13 February 1923. However, cloth cap diamonds continued to be worn by many ranks for a time until General Routine Order No. 55 of 20 November 1923 prohibited the practice entirely. After ten years of transformation, the Volunteer soldiers had finally achieved uniformity of dress.

TRAINING

Right from the outset the biggest problem facing the Volunteer Movement was how to decide on programmes of training that would bring recruits up to a reasonable proficiency in drill, discipline, basic fieldcraft and marksmanship. To this end a General Instruction was issued by the Volunteer Executive in the spring of 1914 advocating that every effort be made to recruit Volunteers who had previously seen service in the British Army and who could quickly be utilised as instructors. One month later a

A brigade commander and his staff uniformly dressed in 1922 as per regulations – complete with mascot. The first corps collar badges also began to make an appearance at this time. (Irish Military Archives)

general Volunteer drill manual was approved and published by Ponsonby's of Grafton Street, Dublin, priced at one shilling. In fact this document was almost a carbon copy of the *British Infantry Manual 1911* but it perfectly served its purpose for those now flocking to the new organisation. Week-night training took place for the most part indoors with classes devoted to foot and arms drill, basic musketry, first aid and map reading. On Sundays the new recruits were expected to sacrifice their days off to take part in route marches to improve basic levels of fitness, and tactical exercises were initiated to develop individual fieldcraft skills and to foster group cohesion.

As the organisation expanded it also became necessary to concentrate units in training camps over longer periods in order to facilitate advanced officer and squad-commander training. In the spring of 1915 both the Central Executive and the General Council debated the matter and agreed to allocate the princely sum of £100 for this purpose. However, it quickly emerged that the necessary camping equipment could not be procured from regular manufacturers as, yet again, these suppliers were already committed to fulfilling contracts placed by the British War Office. Nonetheless, the first Volunteer summer camp eventually took place during mid-July in County Tyrone with two further concentrations held during August in Wicklow and north Cork, with a fourth taking place in Galway during September. On each occasion over 200 men attended and plans were immediately made to develop this concept further.

But most training was still done on week-nights and, while the Dublin Brigade was relatively well equipped with the rifles landed at Howth in July 1914, Volunteers throughout the remainder of the country were generally left to purchase their own weapons. Occasionally fund-raising raffles were

National Volunteers training for their marksmanship certificates at an indoor rifle range in Dublin during 1914. Similar facilities were later established by the Irish Volunteers after the 'split' with Redmond. (National Museum of Ireland)

held in which the first prize would generally be a rifle, but an overall shortage of weapons remained that had a detrimental effect on training and morale. To alleviate this, wooden rifles were frequently used for training purposes and it was not unknown to see squads of Volunteers marching along happily with their painted wooded firearms glistening in the evening sunshine which in turn deceived the RIC with regard to the number of weapons they possessed. Ammunition was also in short supply and when live firing did take place most Volunteers were only permitted to fire two to three rounds.

In the aftermath of the 1916 Rebellion opportunities to carry out 'organised' training became very restricted due to increased vigilance on the part of the Crown authorities. Many Volunteer halls were forcibly closed and training had to be conducted clandestinely, usually in rural locations, with sentries posted to warn of approaching RIC or British Army patrols.

In April 1917 Liam Deasy joined his local Volunteer company at Bandon in County Cork which, at the time, was parading twice weekly in an old disused three-storey building known as the 'Old Dispensary'. Deasy recalled that:

> Each parade began with a roll-call, after which we were instructed for a half hour in the elementary principles of military drill, such as numbering off, forming fours and marching. As rifles were unavailable, we used hurleys, spade handles, or even newly cut saplings for our drill exercises. The only weapon available was a revolver and we experimented with it in order to learn the technique of loading and taking aim.

This situation improved moderately during the Anglo-Irish War when supplies of captured weapons enabled units to increase their levels of basic training, but the entire movement still remained under intense scrutiny from the security forces.

Volunteers from the Cork Brigade attending a week-end 'field day' during the summer of 1914 on the grounds of the city racecourse. (Cork Public Museum)

Prior to the 1916 Rebellion some Volunteer officers carried wooden revolvers while on public parade in order to deceive the RIC with regard to the actual armaments they possessed. (Author's collection)

A drill manual published by the Irish Volunteers in 1917 – *Slí Na Saoirse* ('The Way of Freedom') and *Leabhar Drille* ('Drill Manual'). By this time, all arms and foot drill was conducted in Irish. (Author's collection)

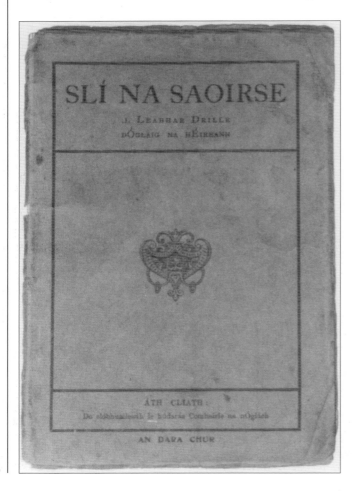

In an attempt to deal with this reality and increased security force activity, in 1920 GHQ ordered each brigade to form a mobile strike force known as a 'Flying Column', and that all sub-units were to combine their limited resources to provide the necessary logistic support to maintain this new formation in the field. Tom Barry, the training officer of the 3rd West Cork Brigade, was one such person appointed to command a column and he developed a system whereby a series of week-long training camps would be held for battalion and company officers. Thereafter, those participating would be mobilised for an operation after which the Column would be 'stood down' with all personnel returning to their own companies. This was an excellent system. It ensured that maximum numbers received at least one period of intensive training and experienced some level of warfare before reverting to normal duties.

Barry's training programme was innovative and rigorous. On arrival, personnel were detailed off into sections and section commanders were appointed. During the camp they underwent a daily period of arms and foot drill, a series of tactical exercises were carried out, and each evening the men assembled for a written exercise or lecture which, according to Barry, 'could not be compiled from textbooks, since there were none which could tell this Flying Column how it could fight and exist in the midst of enemy posts'. His watchwords at all times: 'discipline, speed, silence and security'.

In contrast, during the Civil War the National Army had the 'luxury' of newly occupied barracks and posts (those that weren't destroyed by anti-Treaty forces) in which to conduct their training. They could also avail themselves of the many former British Army rifle ranges dotted throughout the countryside and when recruits joined units that were committed to ongoing operations, they commenced their basic training 'in the field' and refined it later.

Soldiers with previous service as non-commissioned officers (NCOs) in the British Army were immediately appointed as instructors in their area of expertise and by April 1923 courses for machine-gunners, potential NCOs, and cooks had commenced at the Curragh Camp with an Army School of Instruction formally established that November.

BELIEF AND BELONGING

Addressing the capacity crowd at the Rotunda Rink on that famous night in November 1913 Professor Eoin MacNeill declared:

> We are meeting in public in order to proceed at once to the enrolment and organisation of a National Force of Volunteers. We believe that the national instinct of the people and their reasoned opinion has been steadily forming itself for some time past in favour of this undertaking. All that is now needed is to create a suitable opportunity, to make a beginning and from a public meeting of the most unrestricted and representative kind, in the capital of the country, and to invite all the able-bodied men of Ireland to form themselves into a united and disciplined body of freemen prepared to secure and maintain the rights and liberties common to all the people of Ireland.

National Army recruits receive instruction on the Lewis machine-gun at Clonskeagh Castle, Dublin, in April 1922. The large number of personnel with previous service in the British Army provided a very convenient pool of qualified instructors. (Irish Military Archives)

He was quickly followed by Patrick Pearse who set out his own agenda:

> The bearing of arms is not only the proudest right of citizenship, but it is the most essential duty, because the ability to enjoy the other rights and to discharge the other duties of citizenship can only be guarded by the ability to defend citizenship.

Referring to the ongoing Home Rule debate, he went on to say that:

> There are people in the hall who share the belief that for Ireland there can be no true freedom within the British Empire. There are, doubtless, many more who believe that Ireland can achieve and enjoy very substantial freedom within the Empire. But Ireland armed will, at any rate, make a better bargain with the Empire than Ireland unarmed.

These beliefs so eloquently expressed were shared by thousands of young Irishmen who quickly became the backbone of the Volunteer Movement. However, after the split with Redmond, the more nationalist-minded were more than willing to follow the radical leadership provided by Pearse as they embarked on a journey that would ultimately lead them into open rebellion with the Crown.

Later, with the Rebellion collapsing all around him and his headquarters in the GPO in flames, Pearse, the Commander-in-Chief of the insurgent Volunteers, sat down at 9.30 am on Friday 28 April 1916 to draft his final despatch and tribute to his soldiers. He wrote:

> I desire now, lest I may not have an opportunity later, to pay homage to the gallantry of the soldiers of Irish Freedom who have during the past four days been writing with fire and steel the most glorious chapter in the later history of Ireland. Justice can never be done to their heroism, to the discipline, to their gay and unconquerable spirit in the midst of peril and death.

The Easter Rebellion was a testament to the fighting spirit and morale of the Irish Volunteers. Even when faced with certain defeat during the closing stages many garrisons sang out 'The Soldier's Song' in defiance and it was this song, which not only motivated the Volunteers to persevere during their most traumatic hours but also subsequently became the National Anthem of the Irish Republic.

The Proclamation of the Irish Republic as read out by Patrick Pearse and posted throughout Dublin during the 1916 Rebellion. (National Museum of Ireland)

But the Rebellion also served as an inspiration for others to join the Volunteer Movement. Tom Barry, who was serving with the British Army in Mesopotamia at the time, later recalled:

> I awoke to the echo of guns being fired in the capital of my own country. It was a rude awakening, guns being fired at the people of my own race by soldiers of the same army with which I was serving.

Equally, Ernie O'Malley, a 21-year-old medical student at University College, Dublin, had never shown any interest in nationalism. He claims that he had 'heard little of the Volunteers or the various other movements'. In fact when the Rebellion erupted a student member of the Officer Training Corps had actually invited him to assist in the defence of Trinity College, but upon hearing this another of O'Malley's friends told him:

> Remember you'll have to shoot down Irishmen, your own countrymen [if you join in the Trinity College defence]. You bear them no hatred, mark my words, you'll be sorry ever afterwards, think it over.

Over the next couple of days O'Malley thought seriously about what the Volunteers were trying to achieve and he reached his own conclusion: 'They had a purpose I did not share,' he wrote, 'but no one had a right to Ireland except the Irish. In the city Irishmen were fighting British troops against long odds. I was going to help them in some way.' By the time the Rebellion concluded O'Malley had managed to acquire a rifle and to fire on a British position. He had also become committed to the concept of an independent Ireland and later he enlisted as a Volunteer in F Company of the 1st Dublin Battalion.

Others were similarly motivated. On Easter Saturday, Volunteer Patrick O'Connor bade farewell to his family in Rathmore, County Kerry, and boarded a train to Cork City *en route* for Dublin. While in Cork he paid a visit to his young cousin, Florence O'Donoghue. O'Connor was a post-office clerk in Dublin and was on his way back to the capital after attending the funeral of his younger brother. He told O'Donoghue that he had come to say goodbye in case he never saw him again. O'Donoghue was puzzled by these words and attributed them to the effects of his brother's death and the drinking that was part and parcel of rural funerals. He was totally unaware of O'Connor's membership of the Volunteers and would be deeply shocked a few days later to learn that he had been killed fighting near O'Connell Street on the last day of the Rebellion.

The Easter Rebellion and its bloody aftermath, together with the death of O'Connor, had a profound effect on O'Donoghue. Along with thousands of others he now found himself examining the motives of those Volunteers who were prepared to sacrifice their lives in the cause of Irish freedom. In the weeks and months that followed, O'Donoghue devoted all his free time to reading books on Irish history. He also studied the lives of those who had led the Rebellion and the ideals set out in the 'Proclamation'. He later described the Rebellion as: 'an illumination, a lifting of the mental horizon giving glimpses of an undiscovered country,' and asked himself:

What manner of men were those who put their names to the brave inspiring words of the Proclamation? What was this idea of national freedom for which they had fought and sacrificed themselves?

For O'Donoghue the phrase in the Proclamation that said: 'In the name of God and of the dead generations from which she receives her tradition of nationhood, Ireland, through us, summons her children to her flag and strikes for her freedom' was everything.

There it was, simple, inescapable, – something that called insistently to an instinct smothered in us all – and during that summer after the Rising there was a wave of what I can only describe as national pride. A fresh exhilarating wind was blowing in Ireland.

The 'wind' of which O'Donoghue spoke was reflected in renewed interest in the Volunteer Movement. As news of the court-martials and execution of the leaders emerged, public opinion began to shift. Even moderates became outraged and this was later reflected in the results of the 1918 general election when, with a number of Volunteers standing for election, Sinn Fein marched to an overwhelming victory and secured a majority of the seats available to the Irish as Members of Parliament in the House of Commons at Westminster.

Of course not every Volunteer was pleased with these developments. Dan Breen of the 3rd Tipperary Brigade believed that while:

The people had by an overwhelming majority given us the moral sanction to drive the British out of Ireland, the election had a serious effect on our army. Many [Volunteers] had ceased to be soldiers and had become politicians. There was the danger of disintegration, a danger which had been growing since the threat of conscription had disappeared a few months earlier. I was convinced that some sort of [military] action was absolutely necessary.

It was beliefs like these that motivated Breen, and others like him, to initiate attacks on the RIC as part of a renewed armed struggle for independence which by 1920 had reached a high degree of intensity. Realising that an outright military victory was virtually impossible, the majority of Volunteers now accepted that their struggle had become a test of their endurance. This was summed up by Terence MacSwiney, Officer-Commanding, Cork No. 1 Brigade, in his speech succeeding Tomas MacCurtain as Lord Mayor of Cork, when he said, 'This contest of ours is not on our side a rivalry of vengeance but one of endurance – it is not they who can inflict the most but they who can suffer the most will conquer.'

Terence MacSwiney, Lord Mayor of Cork City and Officer Commanding the 1st Cork Brigade, was the most prominent Volunteer to die on hunger strike, thus drawing world attention to the ongoing situation in Ireland. (Collins Barracks Museum)

This concept of endurance was perhaps best illustrated by those Volunteers who, in spite of their incarceration in a variety of prisons, embarked on hunger strikes in order to focus world attention on the cause for which they were struggling. This protest tactic could be traced back to the early Irish tradition of 'shaming' an enemy by fasting outside his door in protest at his actions. It had also been used to great effect by the suffragette movement in Britain.

Among those who carried their hunger strike to the death was MacSwiney. Having been arrested at Cork's City Hall on 12 August 1920 and taken to Victoria Barracks to await court-martial for sedition, he commenced a hunger strike which continued when he was transferred to Brixton Prison. MacSwiney died on 25 October after 74 days without food. His commitment to the Volunteer cause was reflected in his letter of 30 September to Cathal Brugha, the Irish 'Government's' Minister for Defence, in which he wrote:

I feel final victory is coming in our time and pray earnestly that those who are most needed will survive to direct it. Whatever I suffer here is more than repaid for by the fruit already reaped and if I die I know the fruit will exceed the cost a thousand-fold. This thought makes me happy and I thank God for it.

General Liam Lynch, Commander, Cork No. 2 Brigade and the 1st Southern Division, opposed the Anglo-Irish Treaty and became Chief-of-Staff of the anti-Treaty forces. He was killed in action on 10 April 1923, before the end of the Civil War. (National Museum of Ireland)

Other Volunteers were executed for their beliefs during this period, one of whom was Frank Flood, a 1st Lieutenant in the Dublin Brigade's Active Service Unit who had been found guilty of high treason having been captured while attacking a lorry-load of the Dublin Metropolitan Police. His belief in the cause is evident in this extract from a letter he wrote to his brother Sean on 13 March 1921, the eve of his execution:

Goodbye and good luck in the cause. My only regret is to have done so little for Ireland, but this is outweighed by the thought of how much we can do in heaven for Ireland in the great fight.

But the concepts of 'belief and belonging' which had sustained the Volunteers throughout the darkest days of the Easter Rebellion and the Anglo-Irish War were shattered on the issue of the Treaty between Great Britain and Ireland. For Michael Collins and the Volunteers who supported him a democratic decision had been taken by the Irish Government, *Dail Eireann*, and the Irish people. They might not have achieved a 'Republic' but they believed the 'Free State' to be a monumental step in the right direction.

The Volunteers who opposed this development genuinely believed that to accept the Treaty would violate the oath of allegiance they had taken to 'support and defend the Irish Republic', although for many others it was simply a matter of personal loyalty as they followed the lead of their wartime commanders. The spirit of national unity that had previously prevailed now began to fracture. Former friends and comrades in arms became bitter enemies with each side accusing the other of betraying Ireland – and the country spiralled into civil war.

There were, of course, some Volunteers who refused to fire on former comrades. Florence O'Donoghue, although elected to the anti-Treaty Executive, resigned from the Volunteers on 3 July 1922 informing his Chief-of-Staff, Liam Lynch:

> My judgement convinces me that out of Civil War will come, not the Republic, or unity, or freedom, or peace, but a prolonged struggle in which the best elements in the country will be annihilated or overborne. In no circumstances could I be party to a conflict which would bring about such deplorable results.

However, most Volunteers did make a decision to support one side or the other and again took up arms in defence of their beliefs. A civil war ensued which in some families pitched brother against brother and generated deep resentment and hatred. It would take many years for these deep psychological wounds to heal.

ON ACTIVE SERVICE

For the first six years of their existence, with the exception of Easter Week 1916, the Irish Volunteers were essentially part-time soldiers who in addition to pursuing their military commitments also maintained full-time employment, education and normal family life. The average Volunteer received no pay and voluntarily committed himself to a code of discipline that had as its ultimate sanction an ignominious dismissal. Advancement within this 'territorial force' was not rank-based *per se* but depended instead on a spirit of democracy which was completely out of keeping with contemporary mainstream military thought.

The National Army had the support of the Catholic Church who appointed a number of chaplains to the new force. Here Father Joseph Scannell blesses the colours at a ceremony marking the occupation of Michael Barracks (formerly Victoria Barracks), Cork, on 15 October 1922. (Author's collection)

Initially Volunteer officers were elected by the membership and from time to time also de-selected if they proved to be ineffective. This overt democracy was destined to diminish once GHQ had established effective control but it served its purpose in the early days by empowering the rank and file which in turn facilitated the selection of some fine officers.

Routine Volunteer life revolved around the local Volunteer hall which was the centre of all training, organisation, and administration. Thereafter, Volunteers would gather together in selected taverns to discuss the many critical political topics of the day and it was not unknown for such debates to regularly continue into the early hours of the morning. Sport also played a critical role as Volunteers immersed themselves in the varied activities of the Gaelic Athletic Association, an organisation formed in 1884 to promote the traditional Irish games of Gaelic football, hurling and handball. They also took an active interest in the work of the Gaelic League which focused primarily on the revival of the Irish language. However, the lives of Volunteers were changed for ever by the Easter Rebellion and its aftermath, irrespective of whether they actually took part or not. Those who fought experienced the horrors of war at first hand as they put their training to the test in a conventional military setting. Pitting themselves against the might of the British Empire invaluable military lessons were learned, regardless of the fact that the Rebellion itself was something of a débâcle.

The headquarters staff of the Cork Brigade photographed outside their headquarters at the Volunteer Hall, Cork City, in 1915. These halls were the centre of Volunteer activity in the years 1914-16 and the diversity of dress is quite evident. (Author's collection)

The Volunteers who survived understood very well that a different methodology was required and that new strategies would have to be formulated if an independent Ireland was ever to be achieved by the Volunteer Movement. Equally, there was now a growing appreciation of the role women could play in the struggle for freedom. During the Rebellion many Volunteer units received assistance from the women of the *Cuman na mBan* (League of Women) who, although unarmed, had carried dispatches and provided medical assistance. This organisation had been formed in 1914 as a women's auxiliary, and although nominally independent, they were *de facto* subordinate to the Volunteer Executive. However, it was in the provision of support to the families of imprisoned Volunteers that this group came into their own.

In the aftermath of the Rebellion those Volunteers who had fought in Dublin and elsewhere were rounded up and marched off to incarceration in a variety of military barracks and detention centres. With the leaders executed, the remaining 2,519 were then deported to Britain under the provisions of the Defence of the Realm Act 1914 and held in civil prisons such as those at Stafford, Wakefield and Reading.

Later, the majority were transferred to a former German POW camp at Fongoch in Wales, which was in fact a disused distillery supplemented by a series of wooden huts and divided into 'north' and 'south' camps. Accommodation here varied, with prisoners in the south camp housed in the distillery grain lofts, while those in the north camp lived in 35 wooden

A group of Irish Volunteer prisoners in Stafford Jail in the aftermath of the 1916 Rebellion. It was here, and in other detention centres, that the Volunteers analysed their failure and planned the next phase of the conflict. Michael Collins is fifth from the right. (Irish Military Archives)

Irish Volunteer, Limerick City Battalion, 1915

1

2

9

3

4

8

5

7

7d

7e

7f

7b

7a

7c

6

WRy. 02

A

B

Enlistment and training, Volunteer Hall, Cork City, 1915

WRV 02

The evacuation of the General Post Office, Dublin, 28 April 1916

c

The Kilmichael ambush

WRY, 02

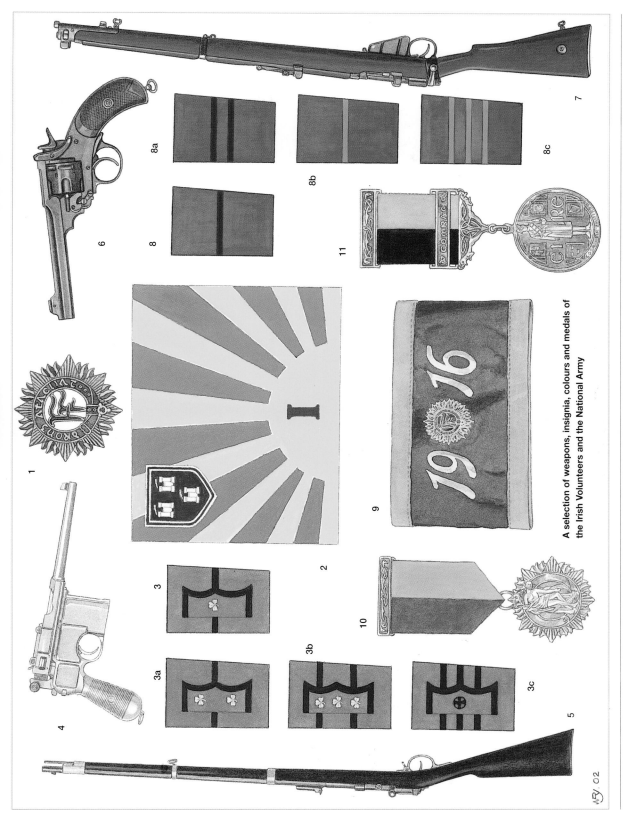

A selection of weapons, insignia, colours and medals of the Irish Volunteers and the National Army

E

A 'safe house' in County Kerry, May 1921

F

After the battle, the Limerick–Waterford Line, August 1922

WRJ. 02

G

1

2

Sergeant, National Army 1923

3

9

First Field Dressing

OCT 1922

7

Best Flannelette **PATCHES** *For Rifle Cleaning Government Size 4 in x 2 in* **AND RUST PREVENTION**

4

6

5

8

H

WRY. 02

huts. All slept on beds made of straw mattresses placed on three boards raised four inches from the ground by two low wooden trestles.

The prison day commenced at 5.30 am with a blast from the shrill steam horn and continued until a final roll call at 7.30 pm. Routine involved attending mass, drill instruction, inspection, a full range of fatigue duties, with time for recreational activity. It was here, during the long winter nights, that the Volunteers utilised their freedom of association to debate and critically analyse the failure of their rebellion. They also determined that conventional military tactics were no longer appropriate in Ireland given the might of the British Army with its limitless resources. Having studied the Boer struggle in South Africa they now decided that a campaign of guerrilla warfare would be far better suited to the Irish context and outline planning commenced to reorganise the movement accordingly. Between Christmas 1916 and June 1917 the majority were released from captivity and reorganisation commenced immediately under the direction of Michael Collins. The first indication that the Volunteers were still a force to be reckoned with came on 30 September 1917 when a huge uniformed assembly took place in Dublin at the funeral of Commandant Thomas Ashe of the Dublin Brigade.

Ashe was arrested for making a seditious speech and had been on hunger strike in Mountjoy Prison where he died of pneumonia on 25 September. On the day of his funeral 9,000 uniformed Volunteers virtually took over the city as they marshalled the crowds and escorted the funeral cortege through the streets. At the graveside a firing party was drawn up, military honours were rendered, and Collins, in a commandant's uniform, stepped forward and declared:

Nothing additional remains to be said. That volley which we have just heard is the only speech which is proper to make over the grave of a dead Fenian.

The military funeral of Commandant Thomas Ashe of Dublin Brigade on 30 September 1917 was organised by Michael Collins and resulted in the largest show of strength by the Volunteers since the Easter Rebellion. (Irish National Museum)

Following this show of strength, the RIC issued an order prohibiting parades, drilling, the carrying of arms and the wearing of uniform in public. Needless to say, the Volunteers immediately decided to challenge these restrictions and on Sunday, 21 October 1917, a series of public parades with Volunteer units in full uniform were held throughout the country. As an act of defiance these large-scale demonstrations achieved their aim. However, they also enabled the RIC to identify who exactly were members of the Volunteers and what positions they held within the movement.

Undeterred, in April 1918 the Volunteers commenced another nationwide campaign when they joined with the Catholic Church and other nationalist movements, in protest against the threat to introduce conscription in Ireland. This continued until the end of the war, but when a general election was called on 11 November 1918 directives were issued ordering the mobilisation of the Volunteers in support of candidates standing for the Sinn Fein political party.

Founded by Arthur Griffith in 1905 to promote the pursuit of Irish independence by peaceful means, Sinn Fein, with a number of prominent Volunteers actually standing for election, marched to an overwhelming victory and secured a majority of the seats available to the Irish in the House of Commons at Westminster. Buoyed by this success, these members of parliament now convened their own separatist assembly, *Dail Eireann*, which held its plenary session in Dublin on 21 January 1919 – the very day a Volunteer unit decided to launch an unauthorised attack on a rural RIC escort.

As these attacks intensified many Volunteers were now forced to go 'on the run' in order to avoid arrest. For food, shelter and change of clothing they often had to rely on a network of 'safe houses' established in each brigade area. These were the properties of ordinary people who were sympathetic to the Republican cause and sufficiently motivated to take the risks involved, knowing with certainty that discovery of their collaboration would meet with complete destruction of their property and imprisonment for all members of their family.

By 1920 the brigades had several networks of these houses covering their entire area of operations and when GHQ directed all units to form full-time Active Service Units these were constituted initially from Volunteers already on the run. Strengths varied considerably with some comprising no more than a dozen, while the Flying Column that fought at Crossbarry in County Cork was over 100 strong. Life was very severe and Tom Barry described the conditions under which his men were expected to serve: 'they had to live rough, sleep in their clothes, and be expected to march by day and march by night'.

Florence O'Donoghue had a more romantic view of the 'safe house system' when he wrote to his wife about his time on the move in Kerry during 1921:

Here the kindly sympathetic, un-effusive welcome of the true Gael awaits you; in every house, rich or poor, we met keen intelligent minds, clean with the sunny freshness of nature. It is a never-ending source of wonder to me, and indeed pride too, to note what a splendid organisation has been beaten out of this raw material in the last few years. No Kings or Princes in Europe could have been treated with the care and honour they bestowed on us.

But not all Volunteers were involved with Flying Columns or urban Active Service Units, which left many more tasked with other duties. As part of the ongoing strategy to undermine British administration in Ireland *Dail Eireann* had also authorised the establishment of Republican Courts but, as no courthouses were available, proceedings were often held in 'safe' locations with individual Volunteers detailed to act as 'bailiffs'. Additionally, the widespread destruction of RIC barracks, particularly in rural Ireland, led to a strong belief among Volunteer officers that the void left by the departure of full-time police would now result in increased lawlessness. To counter this, Volunteers were frequently detailed to act as 'Republican police' and Piaras Beaslai, GHQ's newly appointed Director of Propaganda, recalls how this actually worked:

> Another blow against the British administration was the boycotting of the law courts and the setting up of 'Republican Courts' to which litigants flocked, sure of inexpensive justice, and before which solicitors and barristers appeared. As the RIC ceased to function, some lawless elements tried to take advantage of the situation, and the Volunteers found themselves called to enforce justice and maintain order in the evacuated countryside. Robbers and other offenders were seized and dealt with, and finally a body called the 'Republican Police' was formed and functioned until the end of the Truce.

Initially RIC constables overpowered by the Volunteers were generally disarmed and released. However, once the execution of captured Volunteers commenced in 1920, captured members of the Crown forces were often held as hostages in an attempt to force a prisoner exchange. The most notable example of this was the capture of Brigadier-General C.H.T. Lucas, Officer Commanding, 18 Infantry Brigade, who, while fishing the Blackwater river near Fermoy, County Cork, in June 1920 was abducted by members of the 2nd Cork Brigade in an attempt to force the release of Michael Fitzgerald, a Volunteer officer then held in Cork Prison.

Lucas was quickly passed on to the West Limerick Brigade and George Power, Adjutant, 2nd Cork Brigade, recalled that, 'during his captivity he [Lucas] was accorded the respect and privileges due to an officer of his rank and standing'. When moved to County Clare, Lucas managed to escape and when questioned later by reporters the only remark he made was, 'I was treated as a gentleman by gentlemen.' But not all prisoners taken by the Volunteers were treated with such civility. Persons whom they believed to be operating as British spies and informers were generally executed following summary trials.

With the overall situation in Ireland spiralling out of control a new measure employed was the passing of the Restoration of Order (Ireland) Act on 13 August 1920 which gave Crown forces enhanced powers of search and arrest and enabled the trial of Volunteers by court-martial. If found guilty, Volunteers were liable to suffer capital punishment, and if the trial took place in an area under martial law at the time, the sentence of the court could be carried out by firing squad, as distinct from hanging if the area was under civil jurisdiction.

The scenes outside prison walls on these occasions were always traumatic with large crowds of women, usually from *Cuman na mBan*, joining with friends and relatives of the condemned Volunteers as they prayed for their souls. On 14 March 1921, in one such example, six Volunteers were hanged at Mountjoy Prison and the *Freeman's Journal* of the day reported on the demonstrations outside:

> The subdued demeanour of the people, their anxious looks, and whispered talks were all indicative of the mingled feelings of sympathy and horror in which they regarded the awful tragedy at hand. Before dispersing towards Curfew hour last night, the crowds outside Mountjoy Prison sang 'The Soldier's Song' and 'Wrap the Green Flag Around Me Boys'.

Of course, not all Volunteer prisoners faced death and as the war intensified thousands of others were arrested and charged with lesser public order offences, or simply interned. By the end of April 1921 more than 3,300 Volunteers found themselves interned in camps such as those at Ballykinlar in County Down, Spike and Bere Islands in County Cork, and at the Curragh in County Kildare.

Due to chronic overcrowding many more were lodged in temporary accommodation in places like Victoria Barracks, Cork, where a number of wood and corrugated huts were erected on the barrack square and christened 'the bird cages' by the prisoners. Charles Browne, Adjutant, 7th Battalion, Cork No. 1 Brigade, was one such prisoner who spent from 16 June to 4 July 1921 in 'the cages':

> In the compound were three large wooden huts wherein the prisoners were housed and fed. The place was a clearing house. Prisoners were thoroughly screened after being photographed, and the photo complete with dossier was [then] circulated to each police and military post in the country. If there was any evidence of adverse activity, or even suspicion of same, he was either court-marshalled or interned according to the nature of the charge. If proved innocent he was released but this happened so rarely as to cause excitement when it did. We lived, about thirty prisoners to each hut, talked and laughed, swapped stories with each other and enjoyed our physical exercise by kicking a rag ball around the compound each day. It was difficult to visualise curfew in the streets of the city at 9 pm as each day we were able to continue our game of football in the compound up to 10.30 pm. One wondered who were the prisoners.

When the Truce between Great Britain and Ireland came into force on 11 July 1921, it had an immediate and profound effect on the day-to-day existence of all Volunteers. A programme of controlled prisoner release commenced and once again it was safe to appear openly in uniform. Those on the run no longer had cause to continue and returned to their family homes to pick up the pieces of their lives which in some cases had been completely shattered by the war. All were filled with hope that violence was now at an end. Little did they know that a further and far more bitter eruption was only just around the corner.

As each British regiment withdrew from Ireland under the terms of the Anglo-Irish Treaty, Volunteer units assembled and marched to occupy the barracks just vacated and commenced a new life as a

Military barracks vacated by the British Army under the terms of the Treaty were quickly occupied by the local Volunteers. Here members of the Cork Brigade parade on the square of Victoria Barracks on 18 May 1922. A majority of this garrison subsequently opposed the Treaty and burned the barracks to the ground on 10 August 1922. (*Irish Examiner*)

garrison army. For a time, normal military routine prevailed until the Volunteers also became embroiled in the national debate which ultimately led to civil war.

In the bitter conflict that followed, daily life differed dramatically depending on which side the Volunteers found themselves fighting. For those who chose to stay with the National Army, conditions were far superior as they received training, equipment, discipline, rations, clothing, accommodation and, above all, pay and the prospect of advancement through the ranks.

On the other side, those who rejected the Treaty had no chain of supply, no support weapons, no opportunities for structured training, no financial resources, and were forced to commandeer goods of all description which thus alienated them from the vast majority of the population. What barracks they held they were eventually forced to vacate and they burned these to the ground as they left, pursuing a 'scorched earth' policy designed to deny the use of these facilities to the new National Army.

Ultimately this destruction mattered little as the National Army established its authority throughout the country. Unfortunately in order to achieve this stability they were also obliged to try, and then execute, several former Volunteer comrades who were not prepared to recognise the legitimacy of either the army, the government or the Irish Free State.

VOLUNTEERS AT WAR

The Irish Volunteers experienced warfare on three occasions – the 1916 Easter Rebellion, the Anglo-Irish War of 1919–21 and the Irish Civil War 1922–23. Each occasion saw the employment of different strategies and tactics as the Volunteer leadership faced in turn a different opponent.

The 1916 Easter Rebellion

The 1916 Easter Rebellion provided the Irish Volunteers with their first combat experience and, although outnumbered and underequipped, they

managed to acquit themselves well during the six days of fighting. The Military Council's plan for rebellion envisaged the mobilisation of over 10,000 Volunteers supported by smaller contingents drawn from the Irish Citizens' Army and the Hibernian Rifles. The GPO and other strategic buildings in Dublin were to be seized and a series of outposts established in the city suburbs in order to control the roads and railway lines along which British military reinforcements were expected to travel.

It was also anticipated that many of Redmond's Volunteers would join the fray and that rural Irish Volunteer units would mobilise once they had received a supply of German arms due to be landed in County Kerry. The rural element would then establish a line along the river Shannon and advance on Dublin, capturing or destroying all police barracks along the way. It was also expected that Germany would deploy at least one submarine along the east coast in order to prevent the British from landing reinforcements at Dublin and Kingstown ports. Thereafter, if the Rebellion failed the Volunteers would withdraw to the north of Ireland, link up with local units and embark on a campaign of guerrilla warfare.

But everything was contingent on the successful landing of German arms which had been arranged by Sir Roger Casement who was at that time himself returning to Ireland on board a German submarine. While Casement did manage to come ashore at Banna Strand in County Kerry on 22 April before being arrested, the captain of the arms ship, *Aud*, was forced to scuttle her having been intercepted by the Royal Navy.

When news of this reached Eoin MacNeill, as Chief-of-Staff of the Irish Volunteers, he immediately issued orders cancelling all 'manoeuvres' planned for Easter Sunday which had been intended to provide cover for the initial phase of the Rebellion. However, the Military Council decided to press ahead regardless and issued another series of orders. In the resulting confusion a mere 1,000 members of the Dublin Brigade were the only ones who mobilised satisfactorily as throughout the country further mobilisation was thwarted by the Crown forces and the crucial element of surprise was lost.

Nevertheless, at noon on Easter Monday, 24 April 1916, a 150-strong column drawn from the Irish Volunteers and the Irish Citizens' Army stormed the GPO in Dublin and established a headquarters. One hour later, Patrick Pearse, Commander-in-Chief of the insurgents, stepped from the building and, reading from a prepared script, proclaimed the establishment of the Irish Republic. Simultaneously, other Volunteers began occupying key locations and designated objectives across the city even though the only armaments any of them possessed were German Mauser rifles and pistols, some single- and double-barrelled shotguns, a few British Lee-Enfield and Italian Martini rifles, the occasional pike left over from the 1798 Rebellion and a small number of Webley revolvers which were carried by the officers.

With not a single piece of artillery between them the fighting would be undertaken by infantry alone and in the complete absence of an established medical corps the Volunteers were expected to administer first aid to one another. However, a makeshift 'hospital' was established in the GPO by a medical student, Volunteer James Ryan, with the assistance of two trained nurses, and a few women Volunteers from *Cuman na mBan*. He was later joined by Captain George O'Mahoney of the British Army who had been captured in the city and taken to the GPO. On seeing the wounded, O'Mahoney admitted that he was in fact a member of the Royal Army Medical Corps and offered his assistance, which was gratefully received.

Mechanised transport was equally non-existent and volunteer units had to march from their initial forming-up points to their designated objectives. However, one officer actually did manage to arrange transport for his unit. Marching from Kimmage in the city suburbs to their objective at the South Dublin Union, Captain George Plunkett commandeered an electric tram at gunpoint.

Once his men were safely on board he promptly put aside his weapon, pulled out his wallet, and asked the driver for 52 'tuppenny' tickets before ordering him to drive

The ruins of the Volunteer HQ in the GPO on Sackville Street, Dublin, after the 1916 Rebellion. This building was later rebuilt and has continuously functioned as a post office to the present day. (National Museum of Ireland)

non-stop into the city centre. Like all other units, save those occupying Boland's Flour Mills and Jacob's Biscuit Factory, the only provisions available to Plunkett and his men were those they could carry in their haversacks and in their pockets. When they disembarked from the tram they carried with their ammunition meagre quantities of tea, sugar, bread and a few bottles of milk. Once these supplies were gone they would have to scavenge for what they could find or depend on the generosity of ordinary citizens who might be sympathetic to their cause.

Communications between Volunteer headquarters in the GPO and the various strongpoints being established around the city were also appalling and the entire operation soon became dependent on individual 'runners' who all faced the risk of capture as the Crown forces under the command of Brigadier-General W.H.M. Lowe gradually set about regaining control of the city.

Intelligence was provided to the GPO by individual Volunteers who had been detailed to scout around the city in order to obtain information on British troop movements. Ignatius Callender of the 2nd Battalion was one who served in this capacity and, having made his way to the GPO on Easter Tuesday and volunteered his services, he was detailed to make a survey of the area outside the barricades, particularly the north-western district. He set off on his task by bicycle and in the village of Castleknock came upon a British artillery battery. Cycling alongside he saluted and enquired from a particularly friendly gunner where exactly they were bound for. The gunner replied that there was trouble in the city and they were on their way to an assembly area in Phoenix Park. Armed with this information Callender wished them well and cycled back post-haste to the GPO. It was in this way that the Volunteer leadership put together their intelligence picture of the battlefield.

Religion was also an important issue for the overwhelming majority of the Volunteers who, as devout Roman Catholics, were very concerned about their spiritual welfare on the eve of fighting. Accordingly, some turned to the city's many priests for solace while members of B Company, 3rd Battalion, who were in the process of occupying Westland Row Railway Station, actually stopped a number of priests boarding a train to Kingstown and begged them to hear their confessions. Patrick Pearse was also conscious of his responsibility in this matter and on the evening of Easter Monday a runner was dispatched to the nearby Pro-Cathedral in order to have a priest attend them and hear confessions. Father John O'Flanagan returned with the runner to the GPO and ended up spending the remainder of the week acting as the garrison's unofficial chaplain.

Meanwhile at a place called Mount Street Bridge, Volunteers from the Cycle Corps of C Company, 3rd Dublin Battalion,

Members of the Irish Volunteers are marched into Kilmainham Jail in Dublin after the 1916 Rebellion, guarded by armed British soldiers and an RIC constable. Only one-third of the Volunteers who fought in the Rebellion actually wore a uniform. (National Museum of Ireland)

began to prepare defensive positions. Commandant Eamon de Valera, the area commander, had been ordered to defend the bridge but, as only 130 men from his battalion had mobilised, the maximum number he could now spare for this task was 16. At midday Lieutenant George Reynolds and four Volunteers took possession of the large three-storey building called Clanwilliam House, having firstly rung the doorbell and asked the housemaid for permission to enter.

On the southern side of the canal Lieutenant Michael Malone, Section Commander James Grace, and two young Volunteers took over No 25 Northumberland Road, a terraced mansion whose owners were sympathetic to the cause, having already evacuated the premises. Here Malone thoroughly fortified the building and ordered that a large quantity of drinking water be placed in each room. Further down the road the remaining Volunteers occupied Saint Stephen's Parochial Hall with one taking up a sentry position in an old schoolhouse across the road.

The following morning Malone became concerned about the age of two of his Volunteers whom he decided to send home. 'They are not even 16 yet,' he explained to James Grace, 'and the chances are they'll lose their lives if they stay on in this house.' This left the defence of the house in the hands of just two people, both of whom were only armed with single-shot rifles. With reality now slowly dawning, Malone went off to the battalion headquarters at Boland's Mills where he explained his concerns to the battalion commander. In reply, de Valera unbuckled his own Mauser pistol and handed it to Malone together with 400 rounds of ammunition. 'Sorry I cannot do more for you,' was all he could say, although an additional four Volunteers did actually join Malone later that evening as he settled down to await contact with the enemy.

Then, at midday on Wednesday, Reynolds received word from the GPO that 2,000 British troops had landed at Kingstown and were approaching his positions. Within hours they came marching up Northumberland Road and as they passed Malone's position the Volunteers brought sustained and co-ordinated fire to bear upon them. Taken by surprise, the British withdrew to consolidate, but once the source of Volunteer fire had been identified, an organised attack was quickly mounted. Wave after wave of British soldiers charged the Volunteer positions to be met by volleys of devastating fire, and within a short time the area around the bridge was littered with the bodies of the dead and wounded.

Eventually the overwhelming firepower of the British began to tell and all Volunteer positions were overrun. Malone was killed in the final assault but Grace managed to escape while those holed up in the Parochial Hall were taken prisoner. Clanwilliam House was set ablaze with three Volunteers, including Reynolds, killed, while the other four managed to escape. Overwhelming firepower was critical in evicting the Volunteers from their positions, but their valiant efforts had delayed the advance of the British Army on their main axis to the city centre for over nine hours. In a dispatch issued afterwards, General Sir John Maxwell stated: 'Mount Street Bridge was where our heaviest casualties occurred.' He was right; 234 officers and men had been killed or wounded in the engagement.

But the British advance continued relentlessly and on that very same afternoon the artillery battery first observed by Ignatius Callender brought

Pictured here are four of the nine Volunteers who took part in the attack on an RIC escort at Soloheadbeg, County Tipperary, on 21 January 1919. Left to right: Seamus Robinson, Sean Treacy, Dan Breen, Sean Hogan. All played active parts in the Anglo-Irish war and Treacy was killed in action in Dublin on 14 October 1920. Breen and Robinson became high ranking officers on the anti-Treaty side during the Civil War. (National Museum of Ireland)

devastating fire to bear on Volunteer positions in the city centre. With the gunboat HMS *Helga* now at anchor in the river Liffey, and her naval gunfire also smashing into Volunteer defences, it was only a matter of time before capitulation became inevitable. And on Saturday, with the city centre in flames, the GPO ablaze and abandoned, and the Volunteers critically short of ammunition and food, Patrick Pearse ordered all forces under his command to surrender.

The people of Dublin had not risen up in support of the Rebellion. On the contrary, many now treated the Volunteers with open contempt. As James Ryan was marched off to captivity in Richmond Barracks, an angry mob hurled rotten fruit and shouted abuse. Turning to Ryan, a fellow Volunteer asked, 'Do you think they might let us go?' Ryan took one look at the howling mob. 'I hope not,' he replied, with a wry smile on his face.

The 1916 Rebellion was without doubt a watershed in Irish history, not because it had been a complete disaster, or that the centre of Dublin had been reduced to rubble, but because it witnessed once again the use of violence by Irish Nationalists and a vigorous reassertion of British rule. Battered and beaten, Volunteer units would have to regroup and reorganise before embarking on the next phase of the armed struggle. This process would take two and a half years and would end on the day that *Dail Eireann* convened in Dublin for the first time. On that day Dan Breen and eight fellow Volunteers would set out to intercept a consignment of explosives being delivered to the Soloheadbeg Quarry, in County Tipperary. They had planned only to disarm the RIC escort and then make off with the arms and explosives, but the plan went horribly wrong and both constables were shot dead. Unknown to Breen at the time this attack was destined to serve as the spark which ignited the Anglo-Irish War – a conflict that saw the Volunteers embark on a campaign of guerrilla warfare against the Crown.

The Anglo-Irish War 1919–21

Volunteer Florence O'Donoghue of the Cork Brigade was under no illusions when it came to assessing the relative strength of the forces now ranged against the Volunteers: 'I tried to reckon what was against us – a regular army and police force, well entrenched in solid barracks, trained, well fed, supplied with all the materials of war, the power and influence of all that was solid and wealthy in the community, the long-established machinery of government. It looked hopeless.'

The RIC was still the first echelon of British law enforcement in Ireland. A paramilitary police force, it had barracks in every city, town and village and, with constables who were themselves Irish, they occupied an ideal position to provide detailed information on the activities of the Volunteer Movement. Its destruction became the Volunteers' first objective

Joseph Sweeney of the West Donegal Brigade later reflected, 'we did our best to make life impossible for the police force in our area of the country. We trenched the roads to prevent them from patrolling in their cars and we attacked parties of RIC and burned their barracks.' And it was in this regard that Volunteers who did not possess weapons, or whose age precluded active service, gave invaluable assistance by conducting intelligence work, scouting, carrying messages, trenching or blocking roads, and cutting wires. By the end of 1919 they had succeeded in destroying large numbers of RIC barracks throughout rural Ireland, thus giving the Volunteers effective control over whole swathes of the countryside and, as more and more attacks were mounted, large numbers of the force tendered their resignations.

However, in an attempt to maintain the strength of the RIC, in January 1920 a campaign was begun in Britain to attract new recruits, with a wage of ten shillings a day 'all found' on offer. There was no shortage of applicants from among the thousands of unemployed ex-servicemen in Britain, and the new recruits began arriving in Ireland five months later. An acute shortage of uniforms resulted in the provision of a mixture of khaki service dress and the dark green uniform of the RIC. When the new policemen first appeared on the streets, some inspired wit promptly named them 'The Black and Tans' after a once famous pack of hounds.

Nevertheless, Volunteer units continued operations to undermine British authority and when in April 1920 *Dail Eireann* declared the collection of income tax by British officials to be illegal in Ireland income tax offices throughout the country were raided and Volunteers destroyed all the paper records. That same month 410 abandoned RIC barracks were burned to the ground.

As the war intensified the British Government also sought new means to deal with the Volunteers. The 'Black and Tans' had proved to be undisciplined and largely ineffective, while the British Army, trained as it was for conventional warfare, was finding it very difficult to counter the campaign of guerrilla warfare being waged against it. Winston Churchill's solution was the creation of a highly trained, mobile, elite force which would be capable of striking terror into the Irish, and recruitment for such a force commenced

The .450 double-action Webley revolver pictured here was one of many Volunteer weapons captured from the British security forces. A variant of the earlier .442 RIC model, this revolver was manufactured around 1872. (Captain Tom O'Neill's collection)

By 1920 most Volunteer units had established a 'factory' for the manufacture of explosive devices. This improvised grenade was made in Glanworth, County Cork. (Author's collection)

These Auxiliaries are pictured on guard duty at a military sports meeting held in Dublin during 1921. By far the most dangerous of the Volunteers' opponents, General Macready, commander of all the Crown forces in Ireland during the Anglo-Irish war, described them as 'a pretty tough lot'. He was right. Many of them had been decorated for gallantry in the First World War. (National Museum of Ireland)

in Britain in July 1920. The advertised wage this time was one pound per day plus allowances, and enlistment was open only to former commissioned officers who had seen combat during the First World War.

This new force, the 'Auxiliary Division of the RIC', was commanded by Brigadier-General F.P. Crozier and consisted of 1,500 men who were organised into 15 companies. To ensure mobility, each was equipped with two Ford armoured cars and six Crossley tenders. The successful applicants were enrolled as 'Temporary Cadets', held a rank equivalent to sergeant in the RIC and on arrival in Ireland underwent a short six-week police course at the Curragh Camp.

Initially these too were clothed in a khaki uniform together with a black leather belt and Balmoral (Tam O'Shanter) cap. All of this was later changed to a dark blue uniform with black leather belt and dark green Balmoral cap which gave the Auxiliaries an identity all of their own as they became the 3rd police element employed to bring the militant Volunteers to heel.

A typical example of Auxiliary operations occurred in Balbriggan, County Dublin, on 20 September 1920 after local head constable, Peter Burke, and his brother, Sergeant Michael Burke, had been attacked by Volunteers in a public house and shot with dumdum bullets. Peter, who had been involved in training the Auxiliary Division in the Phoenix Park depot, died immediately, while Michael later recovered from his wounds.

In reprisal, a party of Auxiliaries arrived from the nearby Gormanstown Camp and on seeing their old training instructor lying dead, virtually destroyed the town by throwing grenades through windows, setting houses on fire, and finally bayoneting two civilians to death. Elsewhere, and in anticipation of reprisals, ordinary people frequently fled their homes at sundown and spent the night in the safety of the countryside taking shelter in whatever barn or ditch they could find. Not surprisingly then the Auxiliaries soon gained a reputation for ruthlessness and cruelty which was well founded. That said, no matter how hard the combined Crown forces tried to subdue the organisation the Volunteer campaign continued apace as adjustments were continually made to counter the threat. One such adjustment was the creation of the 'Flying Column'.

Volunteer Donncadha O'Hannigan was an officer in the East Limerick Brigade and early in June 1920 he had made an extensive cross-country journey into the neighbouring West Limerick Brigade area. The plan was for elements from both brigades to launch a co-ordinated attack on the RIC, but it never happened. Instead O'Hannigan marched home with nothing to show for his efforts. However, he later realised the full impact of what he had just achieved:

> Our journey was without incident because we took care to avoid the immediate vicinity of towns and were very cautious when seeking food. Fully armed, we had travelled over 30 miles cross-country in daylight without any great difficulty. It occurred to us that since we had successfully done so there was no reason why a larger number, organised and equipped as a unit, could not do likewise. What we had in mind was an efficient, disciplined, compact and swift-moving body of men which would strike at the enemy where and when a suitable opportunity arose. For the first time we were thinking about a fully committed unit operating in the field continuously and then engaging in a deliberately planned and sustained series of operations.

It was the favourable reports from O'Hannigan which caused Volunteer GHQ in the summer of 1920 to issue instructions that all units should form 'Flying Columns' immediately.

Pictured here are members of the Flying Column of the West Mayo Brigade in typical dress worn during the Anglo-Irish War. The majority wear trench coats, boots and leggings while the column commander, Commandant Michael Kilroy (back row on left), wears his Volunteer uniform. Most of the column carry the British Lee-Enfield rifle with one Volunteer carrying a 'Howth' Mauser. (Irish Military Archives)

Thus the 'Flying Column' began to emerge, working in tandem with the local Volunteer battalions and companies and continually on the move lest they be surrounded by the large cordon and search operations mounted against them. Of all the flying column commanders, Tom Barry of the 3rd West Cork Brigade was without doubt the most successful. Barry recalled:

We never laid an ambush except by the side of the road. The British were more experienced, better trained, and better shots. My Volunteers often had to go into action without having fired one shot in training so our tactics therefore were to attack at close quarters whenever possible. We always fired at the enemy from a range of 10 to 15 yards – there are no bad shots at 15 yards – at that range you couldn't miss your target.

When on September 1920 the Auxiliaries arrived in the town of Macroom, County Cork, the main town within Barry's area of operations, their reputation was such that they were believed to be invincible. Barry claims that this had 'a serious effect on both the morale of the whole people as well as the Volunteers, and he decided to act. On 28 November his Flying Column of 36 riflemen ambushed and defeated an 18-strong mobile patrol travelling in two military vehicles at Kilmichael in West Cork.

This photo of General Tom Barry, commander of the 3rd West Cork Brigade Flying Column, was taken in 1921. He had learned his soldiering skills while serving with the British Army in Mesopotamia during the First World War and was appointed to command the column at the age of 22. (Dara McGrath/Cork Public Museum)

Few of Barry's men had previous combat experience and most had only fired a handful of shots in training, but they still managed to defeat their opponents in an engagement that saw intense close-quarter fighting. Of the 18 Auxiliaries in the patrol, 16 were killed in action, one escaped but was later discovered and shot dead, while the final member was so seriously wounded he was left for dead. Barry lost three men in the ambush but many of the Column were in severe shock after their first combat mission. To restore discipline he fell them in and drilled them up and down the road amidst the dead before marching them cross-country to a 'safe house'.

This encounter had a profound effect on the Column and Barry recalls the situation after he had posted sentries for the night.

When I returned the men were all sleeping in their wet clothes on the straw-covered floor. I looked at them and a thrill of pride ran through me as I thought that no army in the world could ever have more uncomplaining men. They had been practically thirty hours without food, marched twenty-six miles, were soaked through, nearly frozen on exposed rocks, and had undergone a terrifying baptism of fire.

This victory had a huge impact on the morale of both sides and it forced the British authorities to accept the fact that the Volunteers were now capable of mounting major military operations. Other victories followed, with the most notable taking place at Crossbarry, again in West Cork, on 16 March 1921, when Barry's Column, consisting this time of 104 officers and men, inflicted heavy casualties on a combined force of 1,200 troops sent to destroy them and then successfully evaded capture in the aftermath.

In response to these attacks, martial law was declared in the South, a policy of 'internment without trial' was introduced and military reinforcements poured into the country. Therefore, at the height of the Anglo-Irish War the British Army had 60,000 regular troops deployed in Ireland while the combined police force (RIC, 'Black and Tans' and Auxiliaries) totalled 15,000. On the Volunteer side the numbers varied greatly. For example, the Dublin Brigade had a strength of 3,500 but only 1,000 could be armed at any one time, while Tom Barry stated that he could muster only 310 riflemen in the entire Cork county. Therefore, and notwithstanding the figures for enlisted membership, the Volunteers never had more than 3,000 operational troops to call on at any one time.

Urban-based Volunteers were involved in a different but equally difficult fight which consisted for the most part of hit-and-run attacks on individuals and small groups of the Crown forces. Living in areas which were saturated with the various elements of the Crown forces, these Volunteers also had to function under the added restrictions of curfew. The architect of the urban strategy was Michael Collins who employed 'The Squad' to strike absolute terror into the heart of the British administration. Collins believed that 'to paralyse the British machine it was necessary to strike at individuals [because] without her spies England was helpless.' When he received information that a group of agents known as the 'Cairo Gang' (because of their previous experience in the Middle East) were now directing attacks against members of Sinn Fein and the Volunteers, he decided to hit back. Early on the morning of 21 November 1920, Collins dispatched 'The Squad' to eliminate 12 agents in a carefully co-ordinated operation which in one fell swoop effectively destroyed Britain's intelligence network in Dublin.

In a 'tit for tat' response Dick McKee and Peadar Clancy, two of Collins' closet aides who had been arrested the previous evening, were then taken out and 'shot while trying to escape'. The same afternoon a party of Auxiliaries drove to the Croke Park football stadium – where thousands of spectators were watching a match between Dublin and Tipperary – and opened fire. Twelve civilians died and 65 were wounded on a day which subsequently became known as 'Bloody Sunday'. All the Crown forces achieved was to strengthen the Volunteers' resolve to continue their struggle in both its urban and rural contexts. Thereafter, the Volunteer leadership reverted to conventional warfare on only one further occasion. On 25 May 1921 units of the Dublin Brigade, augmented by members of 'The Squad', attacked and burned down Dublin's Customs House, which was the administrative centre of the British Civil Service in Ireland. According to Oscar Traynor, commander of the Dublin Brigade, the idea for this operation actually came from Eamon de Valera, who felt that, 'A big action in Dublin was necessary in order to bring public opinion abroad to bear on Ireland's case.' Although the operation was a success, the Volunteers still suffered very heavy losses, with five killed and 80 captured, but neither this scale of loss nor the ongoing effects of internment and reprisals seemed to have any effect on the Volunteers' resolve. Their struggle was destined to continue unabated until the Truce came into effect on 11 July 1921, thus bringing the Anglo-Irish War to an end.

The Civil War 1922–23

A period of intense negotiations followed which culminated in the signing of a formal treaty between Great Britain and Ireland on 6 December 1921, the terms of which established a 26-county Irish Free State with dominion status within the Commonwealth, and retention of the six north-eastern counties within the United Kingdom. This arrangement was approved by a majority of ministers in the fledgling Irish Government, a majority of *Dail* deputies, and a majority of the people of Ireland, but it still managed to provoke a bitter split both within the Sinn Fein party and the Volunteer Movement.

In January 1922 the new Irish Provisional Government, comprised now of only pro-Treaty representatives (because those opposed to the Treaty had walked out) held its first meeting at the very moment the British Army commenced its long awaited withdrawal from Ireland. It was at this point that recruiting commenced for the new Irish National Army and many pro-Treaty Volunteers were quick to enlist.

On the anti-Treaty side several senior members of the Volunteer leadership refused to recognise the authority of the Provisional Government and on 9 April 1922 formed their own executive, occupied the Four Courts building in Dublin on 13 April, and started preparing defensive positions. Sliding now towards the inevitability of civil war intense efforts were made to restore order and prevent the opening of hostilities – but all to no avail. When the anti-Treaty forces kidnapped General J.J. O'Connell of the National Army and

On 29 June 1922, 18-pounder field artillery guns were used to shell the Four Courts buildings in Dublin. A total of 375 shells were fired into the anti-Treaty forces headquarters during this operation. (Irish Military Archives)

assassinated Sir Henry Wilson, the military advisor to the Northern Ireland Government, the Free State Government now led by Michael Collins, issued an ultimatum to the Four Courts garrison demanding their surrender. This was ignored and at 4.29 am on 28 June 1922 a battery of 18-pounder field artillery guns supplied to the National Army by the city's departing British garrison opened fire on the Four Courts. The soldiers firing the guns had received little or no training before being deployed and in order to aim they simply opened the breech, looked down the inside of the barrel, took a rough alignment, loaded up the ammunition, and then fired the weapon. Employing this crude methodology the first shots were fired which plunged the country into civil war.

Within a short period fighting spread to other buildings in Dublin and a week of intense street fighting ensued before the National Army regained control of the city. The anti-Treaty forces then withdrew to the south of the country and established a series of defensive positions behind a line running roughly from Limerick to Waterford. Maintaining pressure on this line Collins also decided to finish the war as soon as possible and, attacking on the flank, mounted a series of amphibious landings on the south coast.

Accordingly, by the end of August, the National Army had gained control of the main cities and towns with the remnants of the anti-Treaty forces now lodged deep in the countryside and once more adopting the guerrilla warfare tactics they had previously used against the British. But circumstances had changed and Florence O'Donoghue's assessment of the situation was extremely accurate. 'The majority of the people were no longer with them, and their opponents had an intimate and detailed knowledge of their personnel which the British lacked completely. And there was a third difference. Moving below the surface, but inescapable and emerging now and then in strange deeds – heroic, chivalrous, or sadistic – this was [now] a war of brothers.'

Volunteers Tom and Sean Hales from Ballinadee in County Cork were two such brothers who were split on the issue of the Treaty. Both were veterans of the War of Independence, but Tom now took the anti-Treaty side while Sean became a Major-General in the National Army. As officer commanding the town of Bandon in West Cork it was he who met with Michael Collins on the evening of 22 August 1922 while he was on a tour of inspection. Then while making his way back to Cork City that evening, Collins was ambushed and killed by a group of anti-Treaty forces at a lonely place called Beal na mBlath – among the ambush party was Tom Hales.

Without the 'hearts and minds' necessary to support a prolonged campaign, the operations of the anti-Treaty forces were always doomed to fail. The soldiers of the National Army were now far better equipped and their use of Rolls-Royce and Lancia armoured cars, 18-pounder field artillery guns, and a range of machine-guns ultimately proved decisive. They could also rely on support from the church, the banks, and the majority of the Irish people. With no option remaining, on 24 May 1923, Eamon de Valera, the political leader of the anti-Treaty forces, ordered his men to lay down their arms.

The Irish Civil War had lasted 11 months and turned former comrades in the Volunteer Movement into sworn enemies. Though costly, both in military and material terms, the conflict did ensure the commencement of democratic government in Ireland and enshrined in the Irish Constitution the unique position of the Irish National Army.

Britain supplied a number of Rolls-Royce armoured cars to the National Army for use during the Civil War. This particular vehicle, nicknamed the 'Sliab na mBan', formed part of General Michael Collins' escort when he was ambushed and killed by anti-Treaty forces at Beal na mBlath, County Cork, on 22 August 1922. (Irish Military Archives)

BIBLIOGRAPHY

Books

Barry, Tom, *Guerrilla Days in Ireland*, Anvil Books, Tralee, Co. Kerry, 1968.

Bennet, Richard, *The Black and Tans*, Severn House, 1976.

Breen, Dan, *My Fight For Irish Freedom*, Anvil Books, Tralee, Co. Kerry, 1978.

Caulfield, Max, *The Easter Rebellion*, Fredrick Muller, London, 1964.

Coffey, Thomas M., *Agony at Easter: The 1916 Uprising*, Penguin Books, Harmondsworth, 1971.

Connolly, S.J. (ed.), *The Oxford Companion to Irish History*, Oxford University Press, 1988.

Deasy, Liam, *Towards Ireland Free*, Mercier Press, Cork, 1973.

Duggan, John P., *A History of the Irish Army*, Gill and Macmillan Ltd, Dublin, 1991.

Forester, Margery, *Michael Collins – The Lost Leader*, Sidgwick and Jackson, London, 1971.

Griffith, Kenneth, & O'Grady, Timothy, *Curious Journey – An Oral History of Ireland's Unfinished Revolution*, Mercier Press, Cork, 1998.

Hayes-McCoy, G.A., *A History of Irish Flags From Earliest Times*, Academy Press, 1979.

Harvey, Dan, & White, Gerry, *The Barracks-A History of Victoria/Collins Barracks, Cork*, Mercier Press, Cork, 1997.

Hogan, J.J., *Badges, Medals and Insignia of the Irish Defence Forces*, Dublin 1987.

Hopkins, Michael, *Green Against Green: A History of the Irish Civil War*, Dublin, 1989.

Kee, Robert, *Ireland: A History*, Wiedenfield and Nicholson, London, 1980.

MacArdle, Dorothy, *The Irish Republic*, Victor Gollancz, London, 1937.

Martin, F.X. (ed.), *The Howth Gun Running*, Browne and Nolan Ltd, Dublin, 1964.

Martin, F.X. (ed.), *The Irish Volunteer 1913–1915*, James Duffy & Co. Ltd, Dublin, 1963.

Morrison, George, *The Irish Civil War – An Illustrated History*, Gill and MacMillian, Dublin, 1981.

Neeson, Eoin, *The Civil War in Ireland*, The Mercier Press, Cork, 1968.

Neligan, David, *The Spy in the Castle*, Macgibbon and Kee, London, 1968.

O'Connor, Ulick, *The Troubles: Ireland 1912–22*, Bobbs-Merril, New York, 1975.

O'Donoghue, Florence, *No Other Law*, Anvil Books, 1954.

O'Mahony, Sean, *Frongoch: University of Revolution*, FDR Teoranta, Killiney, Dublin, 1987.

O'Malley, Ernie, *On Another Man's Wound*, Rich and Cowan Ltd, Dublin, 1936.

O'Malley, Ernie, *The Singing Flame*, Anvil Books, Dublin, 1978.

O'Toole, Eamon, *Decorations and Medals of the Republic of Ireland*, Medallic Publishing, USA, 1990.

Younger, Calton, *Ireland's Civil War*, Fontana, London, 1970.

Periodicals

An Cosantoir, The Journal of the Irish Defence Forces, 1941–2002.

Papers

The O'Donoghue Collection, National Museum of Ireland.

Interview

Taped interview with General Tom Barry, 1979.

Collections

Captain Tom O'Neill's Collection of Irish Defence Force Memorabilia, stathan@indigo.ie

ARCHIVES/MUSEUMS

Irish Defence Forces Military Archives
Cathal Brugha Barracks,
Rathmines
Dublin 6

The National Museum of Ireland
Kildare Street
Dublin

Cork Public Museum
Fitzgerald Park
Cork City

Military Museum
Collins Barracks
Cork City

COLOUR PLATE COMMENTARY

A: IRISH VOLUNTEER, LIMERICK CITY BATTALION, 1915

This Volunteer wears a locally manufactured uniform comprising a roll-neck tunic of grey-green serge, matching breeches and puttees with brown boots and a soft slouched 'Cronje hat' worn for 'fieldwork'. He also wears a brown leather belt at the waist and ammunition bandolier and is carrying an M1898 Mauser rifle, one of the weapons landed at Howth, County Dublin, in 1914 and distributed to units throughout the country. His dress is an example of how appearance depended on the individual financial circumstances and availability of materials. The tunic differs from that approved by the Volunteer Uniform Sub-Committee on 12 August 1914 in that the green shoulder straps and pointed cuffs are missing. The cap badge (1) was designed for the Limerick Regiment. Made of brass, it depicts a sword belt with an inscription in Gaelic *CUIMNIGID AR LUIMNIG* ('Remember Limerick') – a

This leaflet lays down the Equipment Schedule for each individual Volunteer. This represented the ideal situation, but the reality was significantly different for the majority of Volunteers as they gathered together whatever items they could acquire and afford. (Dara McGrath/Cork Public Museum)

reference to the 1690 siege of Limerick – surrounding two crossed pikes and a representation of the Limerick Treaty Stone. Bronze versions of the badge were also manufactured. The belt buckle (2) again differs from the approved version in that it is made from cast iron rather than brass. The brass tunic button (3) depicts an Irish harp, but the letters IV, which were part of the approved button, are missing. The brass shoulder badge (4) was only adopted by some formations. The peaked cap (5) is of the approved pattern. The yellow piping around the crown was adopted by the Limerick Regiment. As the majority of Volunteers were devout Roman Catholics it was common practice at the time to carry religious objects such as pocket-sized rosary beads and leather pouch (6). The regulation haversack (7) was made locally of white canvas material. In this case it carries a mug (7a), mess tin (7b), knife, fork and spoon (7c), spare shirt (7d), spare pair of socks (7e), and a towel and soap (7f). Volunteers also carried an assortment of British equipment such as this 1908 pattern water bottle (8). An essential item for Volunteers of all ranks was a notebook and pencil (9).

B: ENLISTMENT AND TRAINING, VOLUNTEER HALL, CORK CITY, 1915

This plate depicts a week-night company training session in the Cork Brigade's Volunteer Hall. A group of men wishing to enlist in the brigade stand to the right awaiting the attention of the brigade adjutant who is busy attesting the latest recruit. The unit quartermaster is briefing a new Volunteer who had just been attested on the method of acquiring a uniform and equipment. To the rear of the hall a squad commander is instructing the last intake of recruits in arms drill using wooden rifles. The longest-serving members of the company, all of whom had by now succeeded in buying their uniforms, can be seen cleaning rifles. As real weapons were scarce, great care was taken to maintain them in good condition. The brigade commander is seen supervising the various activities. Notices of forthcoming events together with maps of the brigade area are displayed on the walls.

C: THE EVACUATION OF THE GENERAL POST OFFICE, DUBLIN, 28 APRIL 1916

On the outbreak of the 1916 Rebellion on 24 April, Irish forces established their headquarters in the GPO located in the middle of O'Connell Street, Dublin. At one o'clock Patrick Pearse stepped out from the GPO to proclaim the new republic and two flags were hoisted over the building – a green flag with the words 'Irish Republic' emblazoned in yellow on the left corner, and a second, the green, white and orange tricolour, on the right. By the end of the day the garrison had succeeded in fortifying the building, repulsed an attack by a party of mounted lancers and established a makeshift operations room and medical aid post. However, by Wednesday the GPO was under direct fire from British rifle and machine-gun positions. On the following day the situation began to deteriorate. The heat from the fires in O'Connell Street had become so intense that the Volunteers were ordered to hose down the barricades at the windows in order to prevent them from catching fire. The garrison suffered several casualties, among whom was James Connolly, leader of the Irish Citizens' Army and operational commander of Dublin. Connolly was seriously wounded

---

EQUIPMENT.   Leaflet A 1.

ꜰɪᴀɴɴᴀ ꜰáɪʟ.
THE IRISH VOLUNTEERS

SERVICE KIT.

The following are the articles prescribed by Headquarters for the personal equipment of Volunteers on field service. Items printed in **heavy type** are to be regarded as important:

FOR ALL VOLUNTEERS.

(a.) As to clothes: uniform or other clothes as preferred: if uniform not worn clothes to be of neutral colour; nothing white or shiny (white collar not to be worn); **soft-brimmed hat** (to be worn in lieu of cap on field service); strong comfortable boots; overcoat.

(b.) As to arms: **rifle**, with sling and **cleaning outfit**; 100 rounds of **ammunition**, with **bandolier** or **ammunition pouches** to hold same; **bayonet**, with scabbard, frog and belt; strong knife or slasher.

(c.) As to provision for rations: **haversack**, **water-bottle**, mess-tin (or billy can) with knife, fork, spoon, tin cup; 1 dry stick (towards making fire); emergency ration.

(d.) **Knapsack** containing: spare shirt, pair of socks, towel, soap, comb; scissors, needle, thread, safety-pins.

(e.) In the pocket: clasp-knife, note-book and pencil, matches in tin box, boot laces, strong cord, a candle, **coloured handkerchiefs.**

(f.) Sewn inside coat: **First Field Dressing.**
FOR OFFICERS.

(a.) As to clothes: uniform is very desirable for officers; if not worn a sufficient but not unduly conspicuous distinguishing mark of rank to be worn.

(b.) As to arms: **automatic pistol** or **revolver**, with **ammunition** for same, in lieu of rifle; sword, sword bayonet, or short lance.

The rest of the equipment as for ordinary Volunteers, with the following

(c.) Additions: **Whistle** on cord; **Watch; Field Despatch-book;** Fountain Pen or **Copying-ink Pencil;** Field-Glasses; Pocket Compass; Range Finder; **Map** of District; electric torch, hooded.

Sub-Officers and **Scouts** should as far as possible be provided with the additional articles prescribed for Officers

By Order

The Equipment Order of the Irish Volunteers

Patrick Pearse, Commander-in-Chief of the Irish forces during the 1916 Rebellion surrendering to Brigadier-General Lowe at Moore Street, Dublin, at 2.30 pm on Saturday 29 April. He subsequently issued an order for all Volunteer units to lay down their arms. Until this order was received, none of the outlying positions had actually surrendered, in spite of the overwhelming odds they faced. (National Museum of Ireland)

when a sniper's bullet shattered his left ankle and the limited medical staff were stretched to the limit as they attempted to treat his wounds while under sustained fire. By Friday both O'Connell Street and the GPO were in flames and the position within the Volunteer headquarters had become untenable. That evening a decision was taken to evacuate the building. Here we see the ground floor of the GPO prior to the evacuation. The wounded Connolly has been moved from his bed in the medical aid post to a stretcher on the ground floor. He is being tended by Volunteer James Ryan and one of the two nurses who had joined the garrison. Despite being in severe pain he continues to issue orders. To the rear, Volunteers are trying to contain the flames while more Volunteers engage the enemy at the barricaded windows. Patrick Pearse, wearing slouched hat and carrying his greatcoat, is busy directing troops to a side door from where the Volunteers evacuate the building, having defended it valiantly against overwhelming odds. This plate is based on an original print *The Birth of the Republic* by Walter Paget.

Two wounded soldiers of the National Army are seen here in 1922 receiving attention in front of a commercial vehicle which had been commandeered for military purposes and transformed into a field ambulance. (Irish Military Archives)

D: THE KILMICHAEL AMBUSH

On 28 November 1920, in a classic example of guerrilla warfare, a 'Flying Column' consisting of 36 poorly trained Volunteers with no combat experience, under the command of Tom Barry, ambushed an 18-man patrol of Auxiliaries travelling in two military vehicles. Barry had deployed his men in three sections overlooking a lonely isolated stretch of road at Kilmichael, County Cork. A number of unarmed scouts had been posted to warn the 'column' of the enemy's approach and Barry wore a Volunteer officer's tunic in the expectation that he would initially be mistaken for a British officer and thereby cause the patrol to slow down. Standing in the middle of the road with his hand in the air Barry's ruse worked and as the leading vehicle pulled alongside, he lobbed a Mills grenade into the cab. Here we see No. 1 Section of the column engaging the first group of nine Auxiliaries. The grenade explosion killed the Auxiliaries travelling in the cab, while the stunned survivors struggled to put up a defence. Barry, together with the three members of his command post and No 1 Section can be seen firing on their opponents. When the second vehicle (out of picture) attempted to reverse away from the ambush position, it got stuck on the side of the road and its occupants were forced to dismount and engage the Volunteers. Faced with superior firepower, the unfortunate Auxiliaries were doomed. Of the 18-strong party, 17 died and one was wounded. The Volunteer casualties amounted to three dead and two wounded. This ambush shattered the myth of invincibility that had surrounded the Auxiliaries since their arrival in Ireland and raised the morale of the entire Volunteer Movement.

E: SELECTION OF WEAPONS, INSIGNIA, COLOURS AND MEDALS OF THE IRISH VOLUNTEERS AND THE NATIONAL ARMY

The bronze cap badge of the Irish Volunteers Dublin Brigade (1) was designed by Eoin MacNeill in 1914. The badge was worn in white metal for officers and bronze for other ranks. The 'FF' in the centre stands for *Fianna Fáil* ('Soldiers of destiny') and was suggested as a suitable motto for the new Volunteer organisation by the priest, Canon Peadar O'Laoghaire, after the *Fianna*, a band of legendary ancient Irish warriors. Surrounding the centre is a sword-belt with the inscription *Drong ata Cliat* ('Dublin Brigade'). The circle of flames represents the sun burst, an ancient Irish symbol of freedom, and the traditional battle symbol of the *Fianna*. No particular significance is attached to the eight-pointed star which was included to balance the design.

This depiction of the Volunteer colour of the 1st Battalion, Dublin Brigade (2), conforms to the criteria laid down in an approved report of May 1914 which directed that all Volunteer colours consist of 'a golden sunrise of nine rays on a field of blue' with the number of the battalion carrying the colours depicted in 'crimson Roman numerals in the centre of the golden sunrise'. The regimental device appears on a shield in the top left-hand corner and in this case depicts three flaming castles – taken from the Dublin City coat of arms. The report also outlined both the dimensions and type of cloth to be used: 'the Colours should, in all cases, be 3 feet high by 3 feet 9 inches wide, and made of Irish material, preferably poplin, which is to be had in superb colours, and is well worth the extra cost'. As with the uniform, the eventual shades of individual unit colours depended greatly on the type, quality and dye available to local tailors.

A selection of Irish Volunteer rank insignia as per 1915 Dress Instructions (cloth pattern) is depicted as follows: 2nd lieutenant (3); 1st Lieutenant (3a); Captain (3b); Vice-Commandant (3c). The 7.63 mm Mauser C/96 pistol (4) was a favoured weapon of the Irish Volunteers because of its firepower and capability to be fitted with a hollow wooden stock. Nicknamed a 'Peter the Painter' after the infamous anarchist who used the weapon in the 1911 Sidney Street Siege, London, the Mauser pistol was used extensively during the Easter Rebellion and Anglo-Irish War.

Nine hundred 7.92 mm Mauser M1898 rifles (5) were landed at Howth, County Dublin, in July 1914 and formed the basis of the Irish Volunteers' arsenal. Distributed to units throughout the country, training with the Mauser provided Volunteers with the opportunity to train and fire a bolt-action rifle. While a considerable number of these weapons were destroyed or captured during the Easter Rebellion, some were still in use by Volunteer units during the Anglo-Irish War.

The .45 Webley Mark IV pistol (6) was actually a revolver. Many marks of Webley were used by officers in the Irish Volunteers, members of 'The Squad' and urban Active Service Units. The vast majority of these 'pistols' had been captured from members of the Crown forces. Webley pistols were later issued as standard side-arms for officers of the new National Army.

The .303 Lee-Enfield No. 1 Mark 3 (SMLE) rifle (7) was used by the Crown forces during the Anglo-Irish War and many were captured by the Volunteers. This rifle subsequently became standard issue for soldiers of the new National Army.

A selection of National Army cuff rank insignia as per 1922 Dress Instructions is depicted as follows: Corporal (8); Sergeant (8a); 2nd Lieutenant (8b); Captain (8c).

The 1916 armband (9) was the first decoration given to veterans of the 1916 Rebellion and was awarded at a ceremony held at the Rotunda Rink, Dublin, on Sunday

The importance of organised sport in the daily life of a soldier was recognised at an early stage by the National Army authorities. Pictured here are a tug-of-war team from Michael Barracks in Cork with trophies won during 1922. (Mr Pat Cremin)

21 April 1935 to mark the 19th anniversary of the Rebellion. This armband was worn by Volunteer veterans with civilian attire on ceremonial occasions prior to the introduction of the 1916 medal (**10**) which was struck on 24 January 1941 and presented to Volunteer veterans of the Easter Rebellion.

The obverse of the medal is based on the Volunteer cap badge. There is no inscription on the sword belt and the letters 'FF' are replaced by the figure of the legendary Irish warrior, *Cuchulainn*. The image depicts the dying moments of the warrior who, mortally wounded, had himself tied upright to a tree stump, facing his enemy with a sword in his right hand and his shield in his left. The warrior's fierce reputation was so well known that his enemies were afraid to approach him until they saw a raven land on his shoulder proving that he had died. The reverse of the medal is plain and inscribed '*SEACTMAIN NA CASGA 1916*' ('Easter week, 1916'). The ribbon hangs from a bronze pin-back brooch of interlaced Celtic design. Volunteer veterans of the Anglo-Irish War also had their service recognised when the Service Medal 1917–21 (**11**) was struck on 21 January 1941. Made of bronze, the medal was issued with a bar (as depicted) to those on active service during the qualifying period (1 April 1920 to 11 July 1921) and without a bar to personnel not on active service during the qualifying period and those who were politically active during 1917–21. The obverse of the medal shows a figure in typical Volunteer dress of the period. Surrounding the figure are the arms of the four provinces of Ireland. The word '*Eire*' is spread across the field, while the words '*COGAD NA SAOIRSE*' ('The fight for freedom') are below the figure. The reverse of the medal is plain with a spray of palm around the left edge. The ribbon on the medal with a bar passes through a bronze inverted triangular suspension bearing a Celtic design in relief, on top of which is the bar bearing the word '*COMRAC*' ('Struggle'). The ribbon on the medal without the bar is sewn to a ring on top of the medal. Both versions are suspended from a bronze pin-back brooch with an interlaced Celtic design.

F: A 'SAFE HOUSE' IN COUNTY KERRY, MAY 1921

The success of the guerrilla campaign waged by the Irish Volunteers during the Anglo-Irish War depended on the support of the people. Many of those who sympathised with the Volunteers provided their homes as 'safe houses' in which arms and ammunition could be stored, and members of Flying Columns or Volunteers 'on the run' could be given food and shelter. Here we see a safe house on a farm in County Kerry during May 1921 in which a temporary field headquarters of the 1st Southern Division has been established. The local brigade flying column is seen departing to the countryside having been fed by the farmer's family, inspected by the divisional commander and given the opportunity to receive confession from the local parish priest. The divisional commander, Liam Lynch, and his adjutant, Florence O'Donoghue (wearing cap), are seen planning their route to the next safe house where another unit is to be inspected. The local Volunteer company has been detailed to provide security for the divisional staff while they are in the area and two are seen here being given food. Adjacent to the farmhouse two clerks are drafting reports for GHQ on typewriters while another stands waiting for the divisional commander to sign an operation order.

Throughout the Civil War the British withdrawal from Ireland continued apace. One of the last garrisons handed over was Richmond Barracks, Dublin, which was eventually occupied by the National Army on 14 December 1922. Such occasions generated high emotion and scenes of overt celebration by the local population were commonplace. (National Museum of Ireland/Cashman Collection)

G: AFTER THE BATTLE, THE LIMERICK–WATERFORD LINE, AUGUST 1922

Having withdrawn from Dublin after a week's heavy fighting during the opening phase of the Civil War, the anti-Treaty forces established a series of fortified positions stretching across Ireland from Limerick to Waterford. This plate depicts the scene after an engagement in which a Company of the National Army has defeated a unit of anti-Treaty forces. The superior training, discipline and organisation of the National Army is evident as a platoon is seen formed up and receiving orders for the next stage of their advance, while medical orderlies administer first aid to their wounded comrades.

Anti-Treaty forces are also searched prior to being driven off to captivity, while a Rolls-Royce armoured car provides security in the event of a counter-attack. Successive defeats drained the strength and shattered the morale of the anti-Treaty forces, many of whom soon came to realise the futility of further resistance when they witnessed at first hand the organisation, firepower and determination of the National Army.

H: SERGEANT, NATIONAL ARMY 1923

This NCO wears a uniform made of dark green serge manufactured for the National Army, complete with brown boots and leggings, and 1908-pattern British web equipment. He is carrying the standard issue Lee-Enfield rifle. His rank markings are those authorised as of January 1923 though he continues to wear the cloth diamond on his cap. His cap badge (**1**) has been retained from the Irish Volunteers. The same applies to his tunic buttons (**2**). Unlike his predecessors in the Volunteers, this soldier has been issued with a greatcoat (**3**). Among his personal equipment he carries a box of '4 x 2' flannelette patches for cleaning his rifle (**4**). He has also been issued a canvas kitbag (**5**), button-stick (**6**) and oil bottle (**7**). The Lewis machine-gun (**8**) was the principal light machine-gun used by the National Army during the Civil War. Field Dressing (**9**).

INDEX

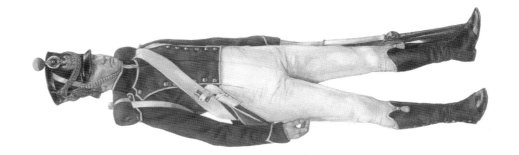

OSPREY PUBLISHING

FIND OUT MORE ABOUT OSPREY

❑ Please send me the latest listing of Osprey's publications

❑ I would like to subscribe to Osprey's e-mail newsletter

Title / rank

Name

Address

City / county

Postcode / zip   state / country

e-mail

WAR

I am interested in:

❑ Ancient world
❑ Medieval world
❑ 16th century
❑ 17th century
❑ 18th century
❑ Napoleonic
❑ 19th century

❑ American Civil War
❑ World War 1
❑ World War 2
❑ Modern warfare
❑ Military aviation
❑ Naval warfare

Please send to:

USA & Canada:
Osprey Direct USA, c/o MBI Publishing, P.O. Box 1, 729 Prospect Avenue, Osceola, WI 54020

UK, Europe and rest of world:
Osprey Direct UK, P.O. Box 140, Wellingborough, Northants, NN8 2FA, United Kingdom

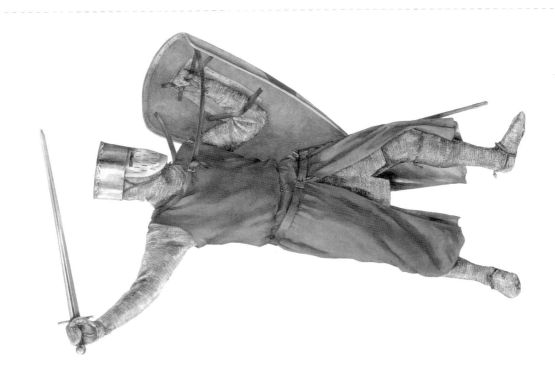

OSPREY
PUBLISHING

www.ospreypublishing.com

call our telephone hotline
for a free information pack

USA & Canada: 1-800-826-6600
UK, Europe and rest of world call:
+44 (0) 1933 443 863

Young Guardsman
Figure taken from *Warrior 22:*
Imperial Guardsman 1799–1815
Published by Osprey
Illustrated by Richard Hook

Knight, c.1190
Figure taken from *Warrior 1: Norman Knight 950 – 1204 AD*
Published by Osprey
Illustrated by Christa Hook

POSTCARD